Be Connected

STRATEGIES TO ATTRACT THE RIGHT OPPORTUNITIES, CONNECTIONS AND CLIENTS THROUGH EFFECTIVE NETWORKING

TERRY BEAN

Chief Networking Officer and Founder, Motor City Connect
Foreword by Chris Brogan

Be Connected

Terry Bean

Be Connected

by Terry Bean trybean.com

Printed in the United States of America

Permission in the United States of America

Post Office Box 30724, Columbus, Ohio 43230
Toll free: (888) 267-7474

Ordering Information:
To order additional copies, contact your local bookstore.
Quantity discounts are available.

ISBN: 978-0-9823332-4-2

A Division of Four Eighteen Enterprises LLC
Post Office Box 30724
Columbus, Ohio 43230-0724

**Book Cover Design By Kim Mettille of
LogoTizeGraphicArtStudio.Com**

This book is dedicated to you; the networkers who strive to learn more, to give more, and to be MORE!

"Once you know who you are and to whom you are linked, you will know what to do."

-Epictetus

Table Of Contents

Foreword: The Network
Is Everything

Terry Bean knows networking. We met a few years ago, and within moments, I felt that I knew Terry, knew what mattered to him, believed from the bottom of my heart that he loved people, and was well on my way to connecting to people he thought mattered. And now, we have it all in a book.

The first point I picked out of his thoughtful book was about one's AQ, your Awareness Quotient. This nugget is exactly the phrase I have needed for a while to explain how some folks can be so clueless.

Go a little further and you see that Terry and I agree that all business is relationship business. He's proven this to me in person, online, and everywhere that Terry's spent his incredible value.

Terry's first rule of networking is maybe why you have this book in your hand: SHOW UP. If you're thinking about networking, then you've done the first right move by putting this information in front of your eyes. You know, Terry's made quite a career from building via networking. And now that you've shown up, he can help you.

What Julien Smith and I discovered through writing Trust Agents was that the network was the most underrated part of most people's business assets. Undervalued, too. What Terry's done here is really brought out the best of what to do with regards to building that most vital piece of your business assets.

One last point: Terry's spent years developing this material. It's worth more than a glance as you rush through your litany of what you need to do to improve. This book, when PRACTICED and really considered, will change how business happens for you.

Are you ready? Can you feel it? I'm there already and I've got shivers. From online to off, Terry's got us covered. Let's use it, shall we?

Chris Brogan, author of Social Media 101.

Opening Thoughts

If I could give you just one piece of advice when it comes to both networking and universal laws of spirituality, it would be simple; ASK.

So many of us find it challenging, as if it's a sign of weakness. Or maybe you were taught that you need to make it on your own. Were you told that others aren't going to be concerned with your issues? That's old world thinking. New world thinking tells us that having the opportunity to help others actually helps us.

We can debate when "networking" commences all day long, but folks in the know recognize the concept of "givers get." Conventional thinking was that those who give a lot of opportunities will receive a lot in return. There is truth to this. What we now need to consider is that the opportunity to help someone else is also a "give." By telling others what you seek, you give them the opportunity to help you. If they do, they have both you and the universe looking to return the favor.

Now that's a powerful combination. It's like they are getting more than twice as much help in return. Multiply that by the size of your network, add your willingness to help, and you can see how quickly effective networking can pay dividends.

This book is all about how to be the most effective networker you can be. I have given a lot of thought, to the how's and why's of networking, since I started doing it 18 years ago. Six years ago I decided to build my business around teaching others how to do it. This book is a collection of my best advice. I have broken it down into five sections:

- Universal Connectedness

- Being Connected before Connecting - What you need to know to start

- Connecting at an Event - How to make your face to face time effective

- Connecting Online - How to make online networking effective

- Staying Connected - The importance of follow up

I put the above in an order that made sense to me. That doesn't mean it will work for you. As you can see in the table of contents of the book, there are a lot of sub-headings that fall under these topics. I suggest you read this book in whatever order feels right for you. Picking a topic and practicing it over the course of the day will get you to mastery faster.

It is my sincere belief that upon completion of this book both you and your network will be far better off. Please share this book and the ideas within it. The more our network knows about the principals contained within, the better off we will all be.

I would be happy to speak to you regarding any issues covered in this book. Feel free to reach out to me via any of the social networking sites or simply send me an e-mail at bean@trybean.com.

I look forward to connecting with you.

Be connected-

Terry Bean March, 2013 http://trybean.com

Be Connected

In order to fully understand the potential of networking, you must understand why Networking works. It is with this thought in mind that I decided to begin my trainings with:

Universal Connectedness

I figure if it works in training, it's a great way to start off the book. I have always held a very spiritual view on how life works. Not just my life, but everybody's. This section will certainly touch on that. Both life and networking are about being connected. When you understand your place in the Universe, you will become successful in having the Universe work for you. Believe me; you couldn't have a better business partner. Since the opening thoughts talked about the power of The Ask, let's start there.

Kicking ASK!

High on my list of most annoying parts of networking group meetings were the "60 second commercial". This was true for a few reasons:

1. If you meet with the same group of people weekly or even bi-weekly, they become very repetitive.

2. Most people spend time talking about what they do (yawn) as opposed to why they do it (engaging) and for whom they do it (useful info one can use to search their "mental rolodex" for like opportunities)

3. Lots of people have no idea how long 60 seconds is. 60 second commercials that last for over 2 minutes are painful.

4. You can't get much else accomplished with a 60+ person group if everyone takes 60 seconds to introduce themselves.

So you get it, I wasn't fond of 60 second commercials. Compare this knowledge with the fact that we never once hosted a meeting in an elevator (so, no "elevator pitches" and it became critical to do something different).

If you look at point 2 above you see other valuable information people could share. I think passion is important for sure. The challenge is while there are lots of "solopreneurs" on the networking circuit, there are many folks who haven't made the leap yet. Let's face it not everyone does their job for love...yet. So passion couldn't be the focus, at least initially.

It made the most sense to get people to talk about who or what they needed to meet.

When you come to a Motor City Connect meeting you have 15 seconds to tell us:

Your Name

Your Company name

Your Industry (if you're a job seeker you tell us the industry in which you'd want to work)

And the one person, company or idea that if one of the attendees could introduce you to today, would make your month.

It's a great system that yields significant results for many people. Mostly because when you're in a group there is bound to be someone with access to what you seek. Sometimes you're describing the person next to you. Other times, you're talking about a person that someone in the room knows well. It's awesome to watch the response someone has when they "have the answer" to someone's ASK. It's hard for us to hide when we are able to help another.

This book has five sections about the ASK and how to apply it. I love being able to help people's efforts become better rewarding by "Kicking their Ask" and I'm happy to kick yours too. Let's get started with why this works Universally.

The Ask - Universally Speaking

You have likely read, "ask and ye shall receive." There is a lot of truth to that. Asking is always the predecessor to receiving exactly what you want. Ever wonder why?

There are many laws that govern the universe. The ones that pertain most to business networking are:

- The Law of Attraction

- The Law of Reciprocity

- The Law of Generosity

If you're familiar with "The Secret,"[1] you have learned a lot about the law of attraction. The concept in the simplest terms is: thoughts become things. [2]

* For the law of attraction - there are three steps to attracting:

1. **Ask** - determine what you want and hold it in your consciousness. Experience the feeling of already possessing what you seek.

2. **Gratitude** - being grateful for what you have is far more powerful than complaining about what you lack. Maintaining an attitude of gratitude allows you to have the right mindset to attract what you seek.

3. **Receive** - you need to be prepared mentally, physically, emotionally, and spiritually before you can receive what you seek.

* The law of reciprocity - is one big reason that people go to networking groups and give leads. The law of reciprocity basically says that as I do well by you, you will go out of your way to do well by me. Simply stated, if I give you a lead, you will likely go out of your way to give me one back.

* The law of generosity - is a lot like the law of reciprocity. The difference is that instead of an individual looking to return the favor, the universe looks to return it. This is where the big results come from giving.

We'll examine these concepts in greater depth later in this section.

Every ask results in an opportunity to give. Of course you don't have the ability to satisfy every need, of every person you meet, but when you can, you should. Why? Because you will be enacting some very powerful laws on your behalf. Oh yeah and it's just really good to help others too ;-)

Here's to asking, giving, and laws we can all live by.

Why am I so certain that *asking* the Universe for what we seek works?

We Are All Connected

"The biggest illusion in this life is the illusion of separation."

I started watching a program called "Avatar - The Last Air Bender" on Nickelodeon with my daughter when it started in 2005. The above quote about illusion is lifted from one of my favorite episodes, when the avatar meets a guru to learn more about life. Think about our struggle to prove how separate we are. We are so different, aren't we?

Look at all the different colors of skin and hair and eyes we have. Some of us have birthmarks or wear glasses or speak in a totally different language.

I think it's fair to claim that our differences are very much "surface dwelling" while our similarities go to the depths of our being.

I have heard the phrase "six degrees of separation" for a long time and I think it is time for us to let it go. It is our false belief in our separateness that creates most of the nastiness this planet now knows.

Be Connected

Picture a world where we all respected and treated one another as equals. Seem like a pretty nice place to live? Interestingly, that's where we are right now. We just don't all acknowledge it as such. I firmly believe that when we all start to believe and practice this, the world will be a much better place.

A few years ago I took on the internal belief that I am god. In order for me to accept that as true, I had to accept it as true for everyone I met. An amazing thing happened, everyone I spoke to became like a god to me. I treated them as I was taught to treat our Father in heaven. Can you guess how I was treated in return? This isn't meant as blasphemous or to put myself above anyone else, it is to encourage you to be your highest self and to treat others the same.

I am not alone in my beliefs about this.

The Shift

There is a movement happening on this planet right now that is unprecedented. Consciousness is elevating. It is happening all around you, whether you believe it or not. It's a most excellent time to be alive.

Let's look at what elevated consciousness means:

In a world full of "conscious" people, we will no longer make decisions solely on the premise of what is best for the individual. We will routinely concern ourselves with what is best for us. And by us, I mean all of us.

This brave new world will be one where, we finally, no longer worry about the differences amongst us. We recognize that we are but one small part of the whole.

The ideology of win-win becomes irrelevant because no one will seek for other people to lose.

With this shift comes an opportunity for you to reinvent yourself. It truly becomes an opportunity for you to live your life out loud and on purpose.

Find Your Flow

I remember watching an episode of Oprah where she made an EX-CELLENT point about people finding *the current of their life* and riding with it. She talked about so many of us who struggle upstream. In fact she mentioned a time in her life, when she did the same. Life can be very tough when we push and fight against the natural current of it. Or it can be a wonderful ride when you finally "find your flow."

Every one of us is here for a reason. We put ourselves here at the exact time we did so we can have and share the experience of being here. The having and sharing all *should* be good. Some of us have been here longer than others. Perhaps we didn't learn the lessons we were supposed to the last time. Maybe it's just that we are here to share with those who are newer to the planet.

Understand that there are times when good doesn't happen, so learn to take the good from the bad experience.

I think of golf as a shining example. There are 87 different ways to mess up a shot. If you look at your ball after you hit, you can always find one good thing with it. Maybe it went 250 yards (and only 100 of them were the wrong way). Maybe it went straight as an arrow (even though it didn't go very far). Focus on that and forget the rest. Why? Because the negative energy doesn't serve you well.

The flow of your life takes place as directed by you. Awareness of the signs that are placed to guide you will often put you in the spot you need to be. If you truly think about what you want and focus on it, you will create ways of getting it. Those ways will show up in your life, pulling you in the right direction. Too many of us don't take the time to pay attention. We keep saying we live in a fast moving world. That's true, but only when we allow it to be true.

Talent and genius only get you so far. My dad did a great job of finding his flow. He accomplished amazing things and grew a rock solid business that still exists 10 years after his retirement. My mother is truly gifted in directing, producing, and choreographing plays in community theatre, but up until 2009 she hadn't transferred that into a sustainable business model. (check out http://www.spotlightplayersmi.org/SPYouth.aspx if you have children near Canton, MI you would like to learn the art of acting). Before launching this, she had spent most of her "professional career" as an executive assistant. If your hobbies have you being the boss, and your career has you as an underling, there is bound to be a disconnect.

The flow is there for you. It's yours. You put yourself here and you direct the flow. Stay attuned to it. Observe. The signs are always there to point you in the right direction. Take the time to understand what they're trying to tell you, because you put them there.

I like living in the flow. You will too.

In order to truly find your flow, you have to work on being aware.

Many of us can discuss our IQ at length. We know the score, we understand what it measures and we may even remember the test we took.

Some of us are familiar with the concept of EQ. It's our emotional quotient or emotional intelligence. This concept basically discusses our ability to monitor one's own and others' feelings and emotions, to discriminate among them, and to use this information to guide one's thinking and actions.

This is all well and good, but I want to know about your

AQ. What is your Awareness Quotient?

Are you aware of your surroundings?

Do you notice even a small amount of the plethora of things that go on around you at any given moment?

Can you dial yourself into the opportunities and signs that present themselves to you all day long?

Raising your awareness is shockingly easy to do, yet very few people practice this. It is a matter of making a conscious and concerted effort to do so. Be in tune with the flow of your life. Realize that your actions can and do have an impact on those around you. Just like the actions of others have an impact on you.

Practice being in the moment you are in, when you are in it.

If you are engaged in a conversation, be engaged. Listen. Listen both intently and actively. Don't worry about what you will say next. If you are paying attention to what the other person is saying, the words you need will come to you without much effort on your part.

If you are playing with your child, play like your child does. Your appreciation of the time will be far greater as will your interaction. It's okay to have fun. All the cool kids are doing it.

Should you find yourself in nature, take some time to get really quiet and listen to the sounds. How many birds can you hear chirping? Do you hear crickets or other insects? Is there water moving nearby? How far off is that semi, rolling down the road (special note, if it is coming right for you, you will need to get out of the way and realize you really aren't in nature at the moment).

If you are writing, let the words move from your head to the keyboard. If you are truly in the moment, they will flow to your fingers as fast as you can type. (Typing skills will vary.)

Realize that there are no ordinary moments. "There is never *nothing* going on." (I love that line that I am "borrowing" from the book *Way of the Peaceful Warrior* by Dan Millman.) Love the moments you live and you will live the moments you love. (I love that line too; I made that one up all by myself.)

When it comes to networking, there is one thing that you need to be abundantly aware of.

Are you nourishing your network so it can nourish you? Networking is a two-way street. I'm often surprised at how disappointed people are with their networking results only to find they haven't really done anything to deserve the positive network effect. It's still work! It's even in the word.

- Are you providing ample opportunity to your network?

- Have you identified both your target client and your target partner?

- Does your network know why you need to meet them?

- Do they understand the value you have to offer?

- Have they referred people to you in the past?

- Are they likely to refer people to you in the future?

As you look through the list of questions and statements, how are you and your network doing? What could you and your network be doing better?

When done properly, networking is effective wherever you are, whenever you are there. As you meet new people and connect your networks, you can be nourishing us all.

There is a chance that networking isn't effective for you. Let's take a deeper look at why networking works.

Why Giver's Gain

Dr. Ivan Misner, of BNI[3] fame, has legions of followers believing that "givers gain." Why? Because those who give, get. A couple of interesting things happen when you give a referral.

The first one is that the recipient is likely to go out of their way to reciprocate. They will be highly attuned to opportunities that would be a good fit for the person who gave them a referral. This is known as the "Law of reciprocity."

The second thing that happens is that the universe bends to make sure that those who do good have good done unto them. If you give a referral to someone, it increases the odds that you will receive one from a totally different source. Some call this "karma." Universally speaking, it is the "Law of Generosity."

How do you make these two laws work for you? Start giving referrals.

Law Of Reciprocity

The law of reciprocity is a pretty simple thing. It helps to dictate how humans interact with one another. The challenge? Sometimes we humans aren't that good to one another. Since we are talking about networking, we won't be focused on those negative times.

The law of reciprocity, briefly stated, says "that as I do well for you, you will go out of your way to do good by me." Is that simple enough? One good turn deserves, and is rewarded, by another.

This is one of the biggest reasons networking works. As you give people a lead, they *feel* almost obligated to give you one back. As such, they go out of their way to do so. It's kind of cool. What makes this highly effective is that they instinctively become attuned to your needs.

Opportunities, for them to help you, show up increasingly in their world. It's like the last time you bought a new car. As soon as you left the dealer's lot you started to notice how many of the exact make, model, and color of that car, there are on the road. This has to do with the Reticular Activating System in your brain. Google it. Or make it even easier and type it into YouTube.

The only challenge is that not everyone is prepared or equipped to help everyone else. This is why we have another Universal Law [3] that really aids in networking.

Law Of Generosity

I love this concept. It is truly on what the concept of networking is based. Many people in networking situations start on the wrong side: they want to know what you can do for them. Invariably the answer is always the same. They probably won't do anything for you, unless they know you will do something for them.

The enlightened networker knows better. They understand the law of generosity. They believe in the concept of *givers get*. Here's the thing, givers can get from anyone. Just because you give to a specific individual, that doesn't mean you have to get from them too.

That's what makes this so great. You can freely give to people that you can't possibly imagine how they can help you, because it likely won't be them who helps you.

Simply stated, the law of generosity says that "as I do well by you, the universe is paying attention and will bend in ways to make sure good is done for me."

Score is kept and hopefully we can agree to say the universe is responsible for keeping it. So two things happen:

1. The universe watches for opportunities that will benefit you and sends them your way.

2. The person who you helped does the same.

Give as much as you can and you will no doubt receive more.

All the networking in the world will be ineffective unless you take Action!

The Power Of Action In Attraction

With the exception of gratitude, I believe that action is the most important piece in the manifesting process.

First you need to figure out what it is that you want to attract. Once you have your vision, act as if you are already there. Use your senses to their fullest to visualize, auditorize, olfacticize, tasteasize, (somebody is making up a lot of words) and FEEL that you already are in possession of what it is you seek.

Be grateful that the Universe has provided for you, just like it always will. Hold that gratitude and let the rest of it go. You don't need to agonize on what you want. If you are, you are likely doing something wrong. If something feels less than right, you need to examine it. The worse it feels, the more questions you should ask. If you determine that you are on the wrong path, change directions. But do yourself a favor, check in with your mind, your gut, and your spirit before changing directions. Manifesting can take time. So many folks change their wants before really giving it a chance. If you know you are on the right path, stay the course. If, after a couple of months, you are not seeing the results you expect, re-examine. If at that point your mind, gut, and spirit are no longer in alignment, review what you intended to make sure it is worthy of you.

The good news is that life is nothing more than a bunch of moments. Each one gives you the opportunity to completely rebuild who you are. Don't carry your bad self into the next moment. Continually live each moment and make it the best it can be. When you take this moment by moment philosophy, you will be empowered to not be so concerned about the bad. If negativity happens in one moment, then you acknowledge it and leave it there. Since like attracts like, being negative will not attract the things you desire.

Truth be told, I had finished writing this entire piece, on the power of action in attraction, through my e-mail browser and my connection timed out forcing me to write it again. Hell yes, I was mad! Mostly at myself because I don't like making the same mistake more than once. (I have made that particular one no less than 7 times this year alone.) So that was a bad moment. In fact, it was probably 3 bad moments and will likely irk me again 2 more times over the next 3 months. But the good news is, I got to make up some words and share a story in this version. It all works out for the best (unless, of course, you neither like my story or my made up words).

So now you are aware that you have to act to attract. You act when you set the vision, you act when giving thanks, and you act in the moment. Your continued action will lead you on a path full of signs. Your job is to be aware of those signs and gauge how you feel when acting upon them. Let's suppose your intention was to find a new partner. Shortly after setting that intention you find yourself speaking with someone new. That's a sign. They could be that partner. If that conversation feels good, continue. You are on the right path. If it doesn't, move on.

The same goes for setting a money intention. If you get a call from a broker, listen to what they have to say. If you have six numbers pop into your head repeatedly, it may be time to grab a lotto ticket. (Actual odds of winning the lottery are ridiculous, even by law of attraction standards.)

If your intention is health related, and you see a new gym open up in the neighborhood, stop by for an introductory trial. Who knows, the fitness instructor may become your spouse and the winning lottery ticket may have fallen out of someone's pocket while they were on the treadmill. Grab them both, sign up for a new membership, and you are the big winner!

What you need to realize is, that when you stop worrying about the HOWs, it will happen. The how is not your concern. You focus on the what, the why, the gratefulness, and the actions required. The Universe will handle the rest. What a wonderful place to live, isn't it?

We are all entitled to a life of absolute abundance. The cool thing is, we can all go after our bliss with reckless abandon, knowing that there is already more than ALL of us require in the Universe. Once we ALL start acting in a manner that is consistent with advancing ourselves as a species, we will soon become a much more advanced species. Funny how that works, eh? We are truly meant to support one another. I appreciate this aspect of life very much and I enjoy meeting and interacting with others who feel the same.

Set yourself up for greatness by helping others get there. If you know the way, share it. If you don't, find it or, at the very least, be open to it finding you. The path is large and is waiting for you to travel it. Trust me, you won't be alone.

The action you take is important for you, but it is important for all of us as a whole, because:

WERALL1

Did you catch the meaning in the section header above? It's an important concept to understand not only as a networker, but as a human being.

Another way the universe and networking are aligned is they support, and are supported by, our connectedness. As we are connected with others in our network, and are connected to the universe, great things happen to and for us.

So many people talk about the idea of six degrees of separation. Stop it! We don't need to focus on being separate. We are separate enough. Consider the degrees of connectedness we have. Here is a hint- there are six.

We will discuss them more in the section entitled "Be Connected".

When we take heed of our connectedness, we are more likely to want to help one another. We also become more comfortable with asking for the help we need. Isn't helping one another at the heart of what networking is all about? Guess what? Ultimately it is at the heart of what life is all about!

Be Connected

We are here to support one another. Great networkers not only know this, they go out of their way to make it happen. What is it that networkers know that compels them to behave like this?

I believe it's the thought behind my subject line. Did you catch the meaning yet? WE ARE ALL ONE. When we work from that premise, the idea of causing each other pain goes away. Better than that, we will focus on helping others because it is really the same as helping our self.

I have shared about how help comes through the universal laws of reciprocity and generosity (see *why givers gain*.) These concepts are what drive networking. And these concepts are driven by our connectedness.

I encourage you to be connecting, be a connector, and most importantly…Be connected.

Be Connected

Since 2009 I've been signing off messages with the phrase: "Be connected".

Sure it's great advice and has significant meaning to me, but does it really matter to anyone else? I think so. Here's why.

To be connected is to be dialed into to the many aspects of life. It's not just that because you have a message from me I want you and I to feel a connection. It's deeper. Much deeper. It's about **awareness**.

There are so many things to which we can (and some of them should) be connected. During TEDx Detroit 2009 I delivered a presentation entitled "6 Degrees of Connectedness" (check it out on YouTube) where I pontificated that not only does 6 degrees of separation look at things backwards, but that there are 6 areas of life to which we need be connected. Those 6 areas are:

Self- This is the part that focuses on knowing who you are

Others- This looks at the importance of relationships outside of ourselves

Planet- Simple, it's the only one we have and we'd better keep taking better care of it

Technology- Without it, you wouldn't be reading this or doing scads of other things you do every day

Universe- Understanding that you are the master of YOUR universe is a key pillar to success

Bliss, although I think I may change this to purpose moving forward- Both of these look at the real reason of "Why YOU are here"

Each topic above has several subtopics included. The video will help lay it out. I have a bunch of audio clips on each sub topic that I promise to share, or transcribe or make into a book at some point.

What are you most connected to right now?

What do you want to be more connected to?

Speaking of connected, there has long been a question about the number of connections a person can handle.

The Universe Weighs In On The Q v. Q Debate

If you have been out networking for a while you have heard the Q v. Q debate. You know, the one that pits Quality v. Quantity. What a strange argument this is.

Especially since the answer is totally clear. Oh, it's not clear? Then read on...

Ladies and Gentlemen! In the red corner, with a reach of over 300 million, we have the "Quantity" camp. These folks believe that any issue can be solved if you have enough connections.

In the blue corner, touting 100% call back rate, we have the "Quality" camp. These folks hold fast to the ideology that your network is only valuable when the people to whom you're connected know, like AND trust you. [4]

A "Quantity" person can suggest many different people, and even more "types" of people, who can help you. They make introductions and pride themselves on being connectors. In their truest sense, they are quick to connect with anyone who has a pulse and can fog a mirror. On some social networking sites they may be a little more reserved on this.

A "Quality" person on the other hand, may not connect with you online, even if you left a lunch meeting together. They are careful about whom they "allow" into their network and, even more so, about whom they refer. You can be assured that if they refer you to one of their connections, action will take place.

So which camp should you bet on? BOTH!!! You can't lose!

Here's the deal. The Universe likes speed.

There are times when you will need to meet new resources

NOW, to fulfill the tasks at hand. Maybe those resources are connected to your "Quality" network. But often, they will be an extension of that network and as such will travel in your "Quantity" network circles.

If you aren't open to accepting new acquaintances, or to tightening relationships you have had for a while, you will miss out.

Before we close this section, I want to share some of the resources that helped me along my path.

Great Books That Taught Me About Living A Networked Life

Two of my favorite books on networking come from Bob Burg. The first book I read on the topic was "Endless Referrals." He really shows us a great path to travel to recession-proof our businesses. He recently co-wrote (with John David Mann)"The Go-Giver" and "Go-Givers Sell More" which are great stories about how giving can really *up* your game.

It's interesting, as I sit thinking about the books I have read to make me a better networker, most of them fall into the meta-physical or self-help world.

I love "The Four Agreements," by Don Miguel Ruiz, and I believe it should be required reading. I think if every fifth grader had to read it, the world would become a MUCH better place in short order.

My first book in the metaphysical genre was "Illusions," by Richard Bach. I read that back in 1992 and it had a profound impact on my life. I was fortunate enough to be telling someone, who had also read it, and they handed me "The Way of the Peaceful Warrior," by Dan Millman. I highly recommend anything that these two have written. They are very solid story-tellers with outstanding messages for all. "Peaceful Warrior" was recently released as a movie on DVD.

"The Celestine Prophecy," by James Redfield, is a wonderful story that really reminds us that we are a part of the energy of this planet. I say reminds us, instead of teaches us, because you can't be taught what you already know. (Even if you aren't aware that you, in fact, do know it.)

"Conversations with God," by Neil Donald Walsh, is another book I recommend. I remember it took me one week to get through the first chapter. It was enlightening, affirming, and really instrumental in helping me create a new belief system.

There is Never Nothing Going On

One of the valuable lessons in the book "Way of the Peaceful Warrior" is that there is never nothing going on. As you learn to live in the moment you begin to realize all that goes on in each moment you live. You will quickly understand that your moment affects the moments of those around you. It is on you to be responsible for the reactions you have to each one. You see, you don't control the moment as much as you control how you allow it to impact you.

I have written numerous times about the difference between responding and reacting. This is just another way of saying the same thing.

As life progresses the one thing we seem to all agree on is that there will be change. In some instance you can affect it. In others, your only contribution will be how you respond to it. Learn to be readily adaptable and you will find greater enjoyment out of life.

There really are only 3 rules of life:

- Life is a paradox in that the smarter we get the more we realize we don't know.

- Its best to have good humor especially when it comes to matters of self.

- And that change is a constant to which you will eventually adapt.

Why not learn these things now and begin to choose the best parts for you?

Life is a play in which you are always the actor and often the director. See you get to direct the effects, but not so much the causes. You can direct the reaction, but not always what caused the action. Realize what your role is and do your best at playing it out.

Be Connected

The fun thing is that your best will almost always be different based on the moment in which you are. Be cognizant of your surroundings and the signs which guide your way and make decisions that will best represent the person you want to be. You do know who that is, right?

It's having a firm identity of your role in the universe at large that allows for the greatest success. Everyone has a gift or talent that others will value. The cool thing is that most times, you don't have to find them. If you put your talent out there and your WHY is strong enough, you will attract the right folks to you.

You can attract those folks at any given time just by being in tune with the moment. Send them good will and prosperous thoughts. You will get them back.

The amount of nothing going on since I started writing this is staggering. It's funny to me how you can be an active participant in the nothing or a passive observer in the everything the moment has to offer. The only limitation put on the greatness of any given moment is the one you put.

It really was a tough choice to decide how to open this book. Most people would have started with the following section. If you have ever met me, you know I'm not like most people

You Before Connecting

Networking doesn't just work because you go to networking events. I see lots of people who bounce from event to event and barely get anything out of it. It's also true that they barely put anything into it. It may be that they don't really understand what networking can be for them.

What Networking Should Be To You

Networking is a lot of things to a lot of people, but ultimately, you need to decide what it is to you. I can assure you that the folks who look at it as an outlet to provide help and assistance to others, do better in the world of networking than those who are running around thinking only about "What can I get out of this?"

Don't get me wrong, you have to consider what's in it for you. Otherwise you will never feel the true effects of it. My suggestion to you is to align your networking aspirations in a way that not only benefits you but those with whom you work/network.

Let me give a good example: One of my favorite things about networking is that I have the ability to position myself as a resource for my clients. In doing so, I am able to accomplish three things:

1. Provide tremendous value to my clients whenever they express a need.

2. Provide value to my network, if any of my clients have a need that my networking partner can fulfill.

3. Be *top of mind* for my clients more frequently and potentially keep a lot of competition OUT.

In addition to being a resource for your clients, other reasons to network include:

Increasing business acumen - You really get to know a lot about business when interacting with multiple business professionals.

Having an external board of advisors - This really happens if you have a formal networking group with whom you meet on some level of regularity.

The opportunities to help others - We, as a people, are really getting behind this idea and networkers do it naturally.

A better understanding of local goings-on -You get to stay current by speaking with people from many other professions.

It doesn't really matter, why you stay focused on networking, as long as you have some strong reasons for doing so. Let's look at some of these in greater detail.

Increasing Business Acumen

When you meet with a prospect, it is vitally important that you display an understanding of how business works. It's even better if you can demonstrate that you understand their business. Networking helps you do both.

If you have a solid networking group, it is likely that you discuss some of the challenges each member faces. In doing so, you gain an appreciation of what other businesses go through.

Since it is natural for people to try and help solve problems, you will also hear potential solutions posed to the challenges being discussed. This information, when properly retained, can serve you well when discussing problems your prospects or clients have.

More importantly, there is a wide array of businesses you will learn about. Traditional networking groups usually have their members give a 10-15 minute presentation about their business. Members will go into great lengths about what they do, why and how they do it and who it benefits. If you take the time to listen to these presentations, you will come away with a LOT of information how different types of companies handle their business.

It is also common practice for networking groups to encourage their members to do a 60-second commercial or elevator pitch. The point of these quick presentations is to teach other members about the speaker's ideal client and business partner. You can put these pieces of information to very good use when speaking to clients or prospects. Especially when you know someone who is a good fit and you make the right connection.

The final piece of this puzzle is when you start meeting fellow members one-on-one. This gives you an even better idea of how to help them. This could involve going to their office, to see how their business runs first-hand. Here you will learn even more valuable information that can serve you in the future.

OWN THE MATERIAL - Find 3-5 people whose businesses interest you, or may complement yours, and set up meetings at THEIR place of business.

So, all that time you sit in your meeting wondering "When will this end?" Stop thinking that. Start paying attention. The information your group members provide you will not only help you help them, but it should help you deal with your clients, too.

A friend of mine once shared that the best piece of business advice he received was that "when it comes to having a board of directors you need to have an odd number and three is too many." I see the truth in that, but we still need some advice now and then and networking can help by providing...

A Built-In Advisory Board

Most people who are into networking fall into one of two categories:

1. Business development professionals (sales people)

2. Captains of their own ship (business owners)

The first group can get you connected to who is doing the buying and on what they are spending money. The second group can share some valuable insight, such as steps to take and ways to avoid mistakes in growing your business. Both of these types can really impact your bottom line.

> **NETWORKING GROUP TIP** Leverage the knowledge of your members. Set aside at least 30 minutes per month to discuss each other's businesses and ways they can be improved.

If you look at the home page of the networking group   http://motorcityconnect.com you will see the two words: Better Together. It's always important to have...

Success

It's like the old saying, *when the tide rises, all boats rise together (I think technically JFK said "A rising tide lifts all boats" but that is less cool)*. Networking is a great example of this. As your network flourishes, most often you get to benefit from that. It's also true that as your business flourishes, your network benefits too. The key is to have the right folks in your network. Those professionals who are committed to growth. Networks need new opportunities to do more than just survive. The people in your network have to be out there making *it* happen. They have to do it for them, for you, and for the network.

Being a good conversationalist is paramount in sales. Staying current is a key to being a good conversationalist. As such, it's no wonder why this piece is so important.

Increased Awareness Of Current Events

Networkers are in the know. They create, and get invited to do, lots of interesting things. When you are hanging out with these "connectors", you'll notice that they are either at meetings or talking about meetings to which they have been invited. Be careful. You certainly don't need to attend all of these events, but it is a great start to get invited to them. That way you can take a look at what's available and relevant to you, and make your choices wisely.

Let me take a moment and define "relevant to you". You should be attending meetings where you will be able to meet:

A. Your ideal client.

B. Your ideal referral partner

C. Current clients (if they invited you and especially if there will be people like them there. See A.)

D. Your next employee

If you're unlikely to find any of those, let's hope the booze is free. Seriously, ask yourself "Why am I going to this"? There is likely a better way to spend your time.

The Ability To Enact Universal Laws

In the section above I explained "why givers gain." Networking really gives you the opportunity to bend universal laws to your benefit. We, as people, are really here to be supportive of one another. For the vast majority of us, that is our true nature. You would recognize this to be true if more of us did a better job of *asking* for that support. **We really don't do a good job of helping others help us.** Effective networkers not only know how to offer assistance, they know how to ask for it in a very specific and concise manner.

The Inherent Selfish Altruism

I love seeing these two words, "selfish" and "altruism," butted up against one another. They seem so contrary, don't they? And yet when you practice networking, you really are practicing the ideology embraced when these two words collide. Networking allows you to get what you want (selfish) by helping others get what they want (altruism). Isn't that cool?

Opportunity to Barter

Of all of the economic structures we have had, I really think I would have fit in well with the barter system. Think about how easy it is to exchange goods and services you have for goods and services you need or want. We can do that with business too. I was speaking to a general contractor friend of mine who has an awesome website. I asked him who did it and he showed me a picture of a beautiful bathroom on his website. I was a bit confused. Turns out the person, for whom he made that bathroom, asked if he was willing to exchange services. It worked out perfectly. Her bathroom got finished right and he has a fancy new website.

NETWORKING GROUP TIP If you are in a group, and looking to grow, make sure you use these "additional reasons to network with us" as a recruiting tool. Be sure to give specific examples of what new members can learn by joining your group.

OWN THE MATERIAL Quick, name three things (in addition to more business) that networking can bring you.

The Individual and the Network

People have long realized the importance of relationships. In the old days we gathered together to hunt, protect our villages from outside threats and to celebrate whatever good fortune came our way. While we don't have some of the earlier opportunities check out any Irish pub on March 17. Seems like the more things change, the more they stay the same.

Many sales pros consider the art of selling a "hunting" exercise. We are always on the hunt for new prospects to become clients, business partners, employees and even investors. The more we cast our net, the more likely we will be to catch what we seek.

Here's the challenge: it's a mighty big world and there are far too many prospects for us to track. It's this reason that has made net-working and relationship marketing so prominent.

I attend a LOT of networking functions and do even more of it online. I continually see folks making the same mistakes over and over. Let me simplify networking to the core.

As an individual inside of a network we have two important jobs:

1. We need to know who we look to meet. Of equal importance is our ability to communicate those needs specifically, concisely and effectively (see this series on The ASK to learn more)

2. We need to know what value we have to offer the network. Value comes from our contacts, our knowledge and our time. Most importantly it comes from our willingness to share these attributes with others.

While they are listed with a 1 and a 2, neither is more important than the other. They are in fact driven by the needs of the individual and the network at any given moment. The more fluid you can be with the actions you take as a result of this knowledge the more positive will flow your way.

Individuals succeed based on the quality of their network. Networks succeed based on the quality of its individuals.

We just looked at the individual's impact in the network. Now let's look at the inverse: how can one individual impact an entire network?

You've no doubt heard the saying "a chain is only as strong as its weakest link". The only difference is that unlike the chain, a network is a living, breathing organism. This is based on the fact that a network is a collection of living, breathing organisms.

In order for networks to thrive, they have to be fed and fed often. Feeding a network is easy. You do so by giving to it. Giving comes in two very different methods:

1. The obvious one is by giving referrals. These referrals can be either helping people who are in the network or by referring people into the network. New people often lead to new opportunities and new opportunities often require new people.

2. The second one may seem counter-intuitive at first glance. It's you letting the network know what you need. Sure that sounds like "taking" but let's look at what you're really doing...GIVING the network the opportunity to help you.

Here's the deal, real networking doesn't begin until there's an implied need shared. Sometimes you're able to help. Sometimes you're not. And sometimes it's you that needs the help.

This is the circle of life of networking. Networks thrive on the actions of the individuals. And when the individuals take the right actions, we can all thrive too.

There are few things more frustrating than losing business you didn't have to lose.

Good Networkers No Longer Have To "Compete" For Business

One of my favorite aspects of networking is that it helps me better serve my friends and clients. Anytime they have a particular need, they ask me. More often than not, I can help them find what they seek. This happened two weeks ago. A friend from college had a sales rep back out of taking the job two days before he was supposed to start. My friend remembered that I have a recruiting background and a large network and asked me to help him. 2 weeks later a guy I recruited for him started. Happy day for the guy with the new job. Happy day for my buddy who got a new employee FAST. Happy day for me who got a nice check out of the deal.

In a business setting, your resourcefulness can really aid you in terms of the customer service you offer. It also can help you keep competition away from your clients.

Let's say you sell copy machines and Jane calls on your largest account regarding payroll services. As she is meeting with the CFO, he mentions how three of his copiers are giving him fits. Jane (who doesn't know you at all) happens to be there at the right time and asks whether it would be Okay if she has her friend Nicole, the copier person, call the CFO. He is at his wit's end, so he agrees. A week later Jane's friend and your competition, Nicole, has a new contract and you have lost a customer.

When you are a resource to your clients, they call you to ask who they should use for things like payroll service. Recognize that if Jane was someone you referred to the CFO, Jane certainly wouldn't be introducing Nicole. That would save you a client. The more of your "friends" and network you can have serving the various needs of your clients, the less likely the odds of someone referring your customer to a different provider are.

It's Okay to tell your clients that you can help them in many areas. Let them know you are there to assist them. It will allow you to forge a better relationship, be in greater contact with them and help out your network.

You saw the part about "selfish altruism," right? Here's a deeper dive into the altruism piece.

Get Ready To Help Others

This is where networkers who "get it" really shine. Although many of us get into networking with the idea of growing OUR business, the folks that succeed realize they also have to help others grow theirs. In fact, many times you have to help others FIRST. **If you can put your needs as a secondary part, of any networking conversation, you will find that most people actually pay attention to them.**

Here's the thing about people, generally their favorite topic is them. When you are in a networking situation, most people can't wait to tell you what they do and how you can help them. Make it easy on them and make it beneficial for you: Let them. Let them get it all out. Allow them to speak and share what they feel they need to about their business. Pay attention, ask questions, and listen to the answers.

This is a very important approach for a couple of reasons:

1. They are going to think you are about the best communicator ever, because they are involved in a wonderful conversation. You know why? Because it's
   about them!

2. This will alleviate the need for them to think about
   what they are going to say to you while you're talking.

You've probably experienced this on both sides of the conversation. You know the drill, you're supposed to be listening to someone, but you are too busy thinking about what you are going to say
next. Guess what? Others do it to you, too.

Give them the floor and they will be more than happy to return
the favor. If they don't, they weren't likely to be a good networking
partner for you anyway. And boy did that just save you all kinds of
time.

NETWORKING GROUP TIP Share with your prospects
that one of the advantages of your networking group is
that you will help them become more effective commu-
nicators.

After You

A popular approach in business these days is the concept of "after you." This is the theory that the other person's needs should
come before yours. By taking this approach, you submit to trying to help others before worrying about helping yourself. While
many in the "networking know" practice this, it is vital that you
remember to make sure your needs are also being met. There are
lots of great networkers who practice "after you" and forget that
after you, comes "me."

One great benefit of this approach is that when it is your turn, you have their undivided attention. So often when we meet people for the first time we are hung up on making a great first impression. We spend time thinking about how we will blow them away with our words. It's very hard to really listen to someone while our mind is busy thinking about what we are going to say next. Knowing that most people go through this, let your new contacts speak first. You are doing them and you a favor. You will spend time honoring them and really learning about them. Then they will have the ability and desire to fully concentrate on you and your needs.

NETWORKING GROUP TIP Being interested in others makes you far more interesting to them than actually trying to be interesting. Take time to understand the needs of your guests before telling them the benefits of your group. It really sets the stage for the reciprocal relationship you both want to have. It also allows you to customize your groups offering to their specific needs.

After you a lesson in networking

We network like we do so many other things...in too big of a hurry. As such, we miss a lot of golden opportunities. I want to share something with you that will change your networking results forever. I call it "After You Networking".

You've no doubt been taught and believe the idea that you never get a second chance to make a first impression. While that is technically true, I don't believe it matters. How often have you met someone who you thought was great and were proved wrong? How often have you met someone you couldn't stand at first and now like?

Here's the lesson: Because of this first impression thing we are in such a hurry to "impress" the person we just met. Unfortunately the way most people attempt to do so is wrong. They do it by talking. They want to tell you all about them. Who they are. What they do. Maybe who they know. And so on. What they don't realize, and this is true regardless of how interesting they are, the first impression is they seem self-centered.

Here's the trick: **Start all of your conversations by inviting them to go first**. Maybe a quick sentence like "tell me about yourself".

Since you know this is people's natural inclination. Let them do it. Give them the go-ahead. BE interested in what they have to say. Enjoy learning about them. **Take time to understand who they are and equally important how you can be of service to them.**

Here are the benefits:

1. The biggest benefit is that you will be able to remember their name. People ask me all the time what the secret to doing so is. The secret is you can't remember something you never knew. We are so busy trying to "impress" people when we first meet them that we rarely even hear their name when we are introduced. This approach allows you to hear it.

2. The next benefit is that you will actually learn about them and their needs. This will put you in a position to truly help them.

3. You will be perceived as an excellent communicator. Why? because you will be primarily engaged in a conversation that they really enjoy. You know, the one about them! What's everyone's favorite topic? That's right ;-)

4. When it's your turn to talk they will actually listen to you. It's true. **They can fully focus on you and your needs because they're not worrying about what they want to say.**

5. You can gauge what sort of person they are. If you listen to them and they don't return the favor, you will know how much future time to invest in them.

Understand What You Seek

I have already mentioned that networking has to start with an implied need. That means about 50% of the time networking is going to start when you tell someone what they can do for you. Do you know what that looks like?

I can't count the number of times I have asked what I could do for someone else and they had no answer. Really? I can't help you with anything? While I would be thrilled for the people who genuinely don't need the assistance, most times those aren't the people we're dealing with. These people are the ones who haven't done the work. They haven't taken the time to figure out what they seek.

And for some that's okay too. Not everyone knows what they want. And maybe they knew yesterday, but it changed. Life certainly has a way of getting in the way. One sure fire way to offer assistance is to help them figure out what they should be seeking. Folks who are ready to turn their lives around take me up on that.

It's important to know what you seek because if you don't, others can't help you find it.

At any given moment, many of us are looking for at least one of the following:

- New information

- New clients

- New business partners

- New job

- New love interest

- New product or service

- New form of entertainment

I am sure there are a few more things that can go on this list, but you get the idea.

Pick which one(s) you seek and tell people. If you need new information on how to use LinkedIn,[5] let your LinkedIn network know. It's as simple as changing your LinkedIn status to read "I have some questions about using LinkedIn. Who do you know who can help me?" You will be amazed at how many responses you get.

If you are looking for a new client, give us insight as to how we would recognize them. Don't just say "I need a new client" or "Anyone with hair. and skin" (Note: Sorry Arbonne, your lotion is awesome. but that is not a good line.) Give us the specifics. The more information you can give us about them – their company, industry, job title, who their competitors are, even their specific name if you have it – the more likely we are to help you find them.

Always remember that proper networking is a two-way street. If you run your networking life solely about what you can do for others, you will find it a very busy job with little compensation. If you are one of the few who either enjoys the non-monetary rewards or doesn't need them, call me. We need to grab coffee.

Acknowledge this: The people who receive the best referrals are the ones who can most clearly define who they want to meet.

Identifying The People You Need To Meet

We do not live in a business vacuum. There are people out there with whom your business has synergies, regardless of your beliefs. Your job is to identify them and form a relationship so you can grow your business. My job is to show you how to do just that.

As you re-examine your years in business, I want you to focus on where your best leads have come from:

- Were they one-time hits or did you receive multiple deals from the same person?

- If the latter, what did you do to encourage them to keep giving to you?

- What sort of position were they in?

- How did your relationship develop?

- How did you give back to them?

- How often did you seek out people in similar positions or with similar relationships?

The keys are:

Understand where you have received referrals in the past and leverage those relationships.

Using the above knowledge, figure out who else can give you those types of relationships and begin creating them.

Figure out who is selling to your ideal client and meet them.

Target Clients

Ever worked with/for a client you just didn't like? Every interaction seems like a wrestling match. Not the Greco- Roman kind, but "big time" kind, complete with body slams off the top ropes. Why is it like that, you ask? It's because you were doing work for someone who wasn't your target client.

There are quite a few factors that determine who your ideal client is and isn't.

1. Are they your type of people?

Some psychologists claim there are only four "types" of people in the world. Others expand that out to as many as 16. In either scenario, there are types with whom you automatically click and others not so much. Do yourself and your business a favor; know your type and be able to recognize them and others.

> **OWN THE MATERIAL** Google: *sanguine* (and read about the 4 personality types associated with this) and then Google: Meyer's Briggs. Take the test. You'll be interested in the results. Both of these exercises can be done in 30 minutes.

2. Is your offering readily accepted in their world? Let's face it you will have a challenge selling PCs to a graphic design studio (any good designer will tell you "it's Mac or nothing.") You need to make sure that what you have to offer is something your prospects are buying in quantity. No sense in focusing on a market that will allow only you to achieve 10% of your annual sales goal.

3. Is your offering readily available in their world? If you have heard anyone mention the book "Blue Ocean Strategy[6]," you know the difference between a red ocean (fierce competition) and a blue ocean (no competition). If you are in a market where you feel like you are clawing and scratching to get ahead, shift markets. Be where few others are and become the dominant player. If the challenge is an industry thing, it may be time to change industries.

Here are some other questions to consider:

4. Are they able AND willing to refer you to more business?

5. Do you have an established history of working with people like them?

6. Is the sales process easy or cumbersome?

Once you have identified your ideal client, it's important to know people who can introduce you to them.

Target Partners

One of the best ways to gain faster entry into your target markets is through strategic referral partners. Having the right partners – the connected ones who service their clients well – will yield big dividends for you. Here are some thoughts to help you discern the partners you seek:

Are they selling to your same decision maker?

This one is both obvious and often overlooked. Let's look at the IT space. Most companies sell to the CIO but also require buy-in from the CFO. If your company sells network security and my company sells data storage, we could meet and talk about the customers we have and the prospects we hope to land. Invariably, we will run into opportunities to help each other, if we are both open to it.

Quick case study from networking events:

I can't tell you how many people I hear who want to partner with Certified Public Accountants. It happens at least twice in ev-

ery meeting I attend. What I rarely ever hear is someone saying "I have some good relationships there, let's compare notes."
Wouldn't that be easier? Why should two people be looking to
forge relationships with new prospects when they could just share
their existing ones, in effect doubling what they have?

What about partnering with companies that can make your offering more robust?

This is kind of the peanut butter and chocolate approach. There are
lots of companies that sell office cleaning services just like there
are companies that sell office supplies. Both of these companies
benefit from knowing property managers, commercial realtors,
interior designers, office furniture companies – I could go on
and on. The key is that their services are necessary and have the
slightest overlap.

Does your customer need someone else's product in order to maximize return on investment when buying yours?

You had better be able to make some referrals. Real estate is a
great example. There just aren't a lot of cash buyers these days
(outside of investors of course). If I were selling houses, you can
bet that I would have at least three different mortgage lenders to
whom I would feed leads. Why? Because having only one is very
limiting to my customers AND to my referral stream!

Time for a little homework. Seriously, do the work.

1. Identify the decision makers to whom you frequently sell. Make a list of five of them.

2. Who do you know who is selling to these same peo-

ple? (Do not name people in your office.)

3. Are you looking to meet CPAs? Of course you are. You know lots of other people who are too. Partner with them.

4. What other products or services do your customers need to make yours work better? Have people in mind to refer. Go to lunch or coffee with them and make sure they're the right type of people for you AND your clients.

5. Compile a list of at least five people in each category as a partner. If you don't know five, call me. I will help. I'm serious.

6. Ask your clients who their favorite vendors are, that sell complementary products to yours. Then ask them for an introduction to the right ones.

NETWORKING GROUP TIP Get the list of your member's target partners created *ASAP*. Figure out who needs to be invited to join your group. Work together and bring in the best possible people for the open roles.

To be effective, we need to have a strategy that answers:

Where Are You Networking?

There are tons of online networking groups. There may be even more that meet in the real world. How does one leverage their networking time most effectively?

You need a solid strategy. It should be built around what you want to achieve from your efforts. I'm hoping by now you have figured out what you seek out of networking. If you haven't, come back and read this when you know what your goals are (Read **"Understand what you seek"** and **"Identifying the people you need to meet"** both in section 2). Getting what you want out of networking is almost as important as making sure others get what they seek.

Is your goal to build quality, long-term relationships, in a specific geography? Then maybe a structured group like BNI o r Amspirit Business Connections (http://amspirit.com) is right for you. They meet weekly, have year-long memberships, and allow you to really get to know the people in your chapter. There are other business networking groups like Vistage and EO who cater to CEO's and owners of companies. Many chambers of commerce offer frequent networking opportunities as well.

When it comes to "face to face" networking, you will want to attend two or three meetings before making a decision. You'll want to make sure the group is right for you and often times, the group will want to make sure you're right for them. You'll appreciate this screening process when you're a member even more. Wasn't it Groucho Mark who quipped "I refuse to join any club that would have me as a member"?

What if you want to meet people all over the world? Then you need to look at online networking sites. LinkedIn, Twitter and Facebook allow you to connect with people everywhere. The nice thing is these tools allow you to strengthen relationships with people who are 3 blocks away just as easily as you can build relationships with people halfway around the globe. Don't worry, we have a whole section dedicated to "You connecting online".

Those are the two primary paths available to you, so how do you best travel them? I can't answer that for you without knowing your specific intentions. But read on.

Be Connected

Ever wonder what's important in business these days?

All Business Is Relationship Business

All business is relationship business. It's that important that you had to read it twice!

Don't believe me? Start walking up and down the street and try to sell anything you have to people you just met. If you're lucky, you have something they want to buy. But if you don't establish a proper relationship, where they feel they can trust you, there will be no sale.

Great salespeople don't sell anything. They make sure they go through a proper process that involves building a relationship and getting their prospect to tell them where their "pain" is. If done properly, the sales-rep "prescribes" the solution. Mike Morley once described the sales process exceptionally well when he compared it to a visit to the Doctor.

You go in. You meet the prospect. You exhibit good bedside manner by establishing a nice rapport. You ask good questions and listen intently to best diagnose the situation and then provide the remedy.

Good doctors can always recommend a prescription. Great doctors always refer you to the most qualified person they know who can best satisfy your needs. Then they focus on the core of their practice.

I'll be honest…I haven't run the math on this. Maybe it's squared, maybe it's cubed, maybe it's quintupled, All I know for sure is shared rhymes better with squared than any other choice. Let me explain what I mean.

Just because you can offer a solution, there might be times when it is better to refer the relationship along. There are so many businesses that have lost their focus so as to be able to cater to their client's needs. **Think how powerful your company would be if you simply focused on one or two core areas and referred the rest of the business on.**

Two things happen:

1. Your company becomes known as **the** expert in those one or two niches.

2. You create multiple referral partners which ideally become multiple new streams of business. You are effectively creating more relationships which ideally add to your reach in getting new business.

Networking has a mathematical side to it.

The Network Effect Of Connectedness

Business transactions take place simply based on relationships. If you have good relationships with many of the right people, you will have more business. It's really that simple (this does suppose that you offer a product or service people are willing to buy).

People network because they know it's a great way to meet lots of new people. Each person is the center of their sphere of influence. Most folks have an average of 250 other people in their sphere.

Think about what it means to build relationships with just 10 new people. Suddenly, you have access to 2,500 new people that you wouldn't have otherwise. Imagine how quickly that number grows as you continue to network and meet new people.

As you are meeting new people, it's important to find out how you can help them. Equally important is letting them know how they can help you. This is where you leverage the relationships you have to create the relationships you need.

It all begins with asking:

- How can I help you?

- Can you help me find a client who desires X?

As you continue to ask these questions, the network effect of connectedness will become obvious.

NETWORKING GROUP TIP Know your true numbers. Think about all of the relationships each person in the group has. Use, the network effect of your group, as a reason others would want to join it.

Your ability to create new relationships quickly is determined by your ability to establish the following quickly.

Networking is really all about relationships. One thing you will notice about every single relationship you have is that you have something in common:

- Family

- You live in the same area

- Work together

- Went to school together

- Same favorite restaurant or types of food

- And any of about 5,000 other things that you both have experienced

Relationships that have these common ties bind more quickly than those that don't.

So how do you find out what interests or history others have that you may share?

Ask them questions, of course. If not appropriate, tell them the "big events" in your life. Either way, the topics should include:

• Where did you grow up and go to high school?

• Where (or did) you go to college?

• In what line of work are you?

- Are you married?

- Where do you live now?

- Do you have children?

- Do you or they play sports?

- What are your favorite foods?

Answers to these questions will uncover things you both share: friends, teachers, common customers, marital stories, sports, and so on.

People generally like people who they perceive are like them.

The more commonality you share, the closer you are to forming a relationship. And it's the relationship that gets business now. It's no longer the other way around.

> **NETWORKING GROUP TIP** Create a bio of each of your members and use it as a handout. Instead of just focusing on their current business, add a little history to it. Use it to help guests uncover common ground.

I've already mentioned the importance of conversing as a skill.

Think about the last time you found someone fascinating during a conversation. What was the main point of the discussion? How many people were involved? Was the individual with whom you were speaking talking about negative things or positive things? Better yet, do you remember what they were discussing? Interestingly, the people we find fascinating are those who have one of two types of conversation styles:

1. They are pontificating or philosophizing on big ideas. (for a mess of BIG Ideas, go to http://ted.com and watch the videos there)

2. They are talking about a topic that is near and dear to us.

Let's look at No. 2. When we talk about a topic that is near and dear to us, there is one that really stands out. It is us, or in this case, YOU. Have you been part of a conversation when someone was generally interested in getting to know you? It's fascinating if someone is asking insightful questions and then actually taking the time to listen. What's really entertaining is when someone takes the time to help you frame your opinions on certain issues by asking such good questions. Psychologists do this all the time. Gifted sales people, life/business coaches, and naturally inquisitive folks all have this ability.

Become a better networker; **worry about being interested prior to being interesting**. I promise you that by taking the time to learn about others through asking good questions and actively listening to the answers, you will become a highly revered conversationalist.

Step 0 in becoming a better conversationalist is to master the art of questioning.

Questions keep the conversations moving. Insightful questions help you learn a lot about the topic. It's important to use your questions wisely as they are the green lights for others to feel good about you.

You can use questions to turn the conversation in any direction you choose. You want to know about the past, ask where they went to high school. You want to know about what kind of friends someone has, ask them about the last house party they hosted/attended. Want to know about their work, ask how they spent their Tuesday.

Open-ended questions yield more results. Questions that can be answered with a yes or no are considered close- ended questions. Open-ended questions draw longer responses out of people.

I have a rule. *I can ask anyone any question I choose. It is up to them to decide whether or not they want to answer.* When I am about to ask a tough or personal question, I share this philosophy to soften it a little. It's as simple as saying "I've always felt that you can ask anyone anything and it's up to them to answer it. Speaking of, mind if I ask you a question?". They'll almost always agree to letting you ask it. Whether or not they answer is a different story.

Ever notice what type of people use questions effectively to succeed in their career? Doctors, lawyers, psychologists, interviewers, and business coaches have to ask great questions. Do you think this is a coincidence? Me neither.

Once they ask the right questions, there is another step they have to take.

Listen Actively

I had to make asking questions step 0 because listening is definitely step 1.

Worried about what you're going to say next? Don't be. Afraid you only have 30 seconds to make a great first impression? While I am not sure of the exact amount of time, I know it's short. Want to know the best way to impress the person with whom you are speaking? Honor them. And you do that simply by actively listening to them.

The best active listeners take what you say, put it in their own words, and confirm mutual understanding. How often do we say things that seem clear to both parties but end up as a miscommunication? Both parties lose out.

Gary Evans, a college professor of mine, always said "Words don't mean, people mean." This means that if you don't fully understand the intent behind the words I use, you don't really understand what I said. We have to dig in a little bit to what was said. It's not enough to take the words spoken at face value.

We've all heard the response "fine" when we ask how someone is. And we can almost tell whether or not they're really fine. Active listening creates a higher level of understanding and can confirm that "fine" (or any other answer) for us.

As it pertains to networking, understanding a person's needs and what you can do for them is the first thing on which you should focus. It is also the catalyst for people being interested in you. You ask these questions enough, you're bound to get people who answer you.

You will soon be collecting a lot of data. How will you handle it?

Cerebral Cortex in Cerebellum Or Customer Relations Manager?

While meeting people is an important part of networking, recalling the right people at the right time is what makes networking really sing.

Just like in every aspect of life, you have choices. You have the ability to remember all of your contacts (Great plan for folks with photographic memories who can also remember names or for reluctant networkers who don't plan on meeting a lot of people.) There are lots of tips and tricks to remembering the people you just met.

OWN THE MATERIAL Google "how do I remember people's names"

Some sort of contact management system is a necessity for those of us who can't remember names, faces, AND want to meet a bunch of people.

When you are an active networker, you likely will gather a lot of cards. What will you do with them? Believe me when I tell you, gathering and placing them on/near your desk is not an effective strategy.

Lots of people use different software platforms. These range from ACT to Sugar and tons in between. Some are designed for single users, other tools can be shared between a few people, and some contact management systems are designed as part of a plug-in for huge enterprise resource planning systems.

They all have something in common: garbage in/garbage out. It doesn't really matter how sophisticated your system is if you don't put the data in the right way.[7]

Having a Contact Management Process

If you plan on going to one networking event a week, you need to plan on gathering at least 20 new contacts a month. Some of you will gather over 150 cards in that time. It is important to note the difference between cards and contacts. You will need a plan for how to handle each.

To handle the cards, you will either want to:

1. Set aside time daily or weekly to input them into some usable fashion. (You're about to be a big-time networker... the shoe box doesn't work anymore.)

2. Invest in a card scanner for you, or someone you hire, to input cards.

3. Outsource this important but laborious task. (Note: Make good notes on the card so your data entry person can add valuable information to your database. Notes should include: where you met, who introduced you, what you discussed, synergies to explore and next steps).

Once you have the cards in your system, it's time to categorize them. Make sure the information is searchable by:

-Industry

-Position/title

-Location

-Name

-Company

This will help you assist your network more efficiently.

Now you need to identify "Contacts." These are people you connect with on a regular basis. You want to know how often you need to reach out to them. There are some people in your network with whom you will communicate daily or a couple of times a week. There are others where a monthly note from you is good, and still others where annual contact is appropriate. It really all depends on the amount of collaboration you are doing.

Understand what your need for communication is with the people in your network and set the alarm in your contact management tool. The more you can put this process on auto pilot, the better you will be at it. This will help you remain top of mind with your network.

So what is your contact management tool? That depends. Is it your choice to make?

Many companies use www.salesforce.com. Others use Sugar, ACT, or Goldmine. I know lots of people that use Plaxo, LinkedIn, or smaller online tools. Of course, there are still people cramming this info into Excel, Access, and Outlook. The key isn't what tool you use, it's that you use it well.

Is the information easy to input?

Do you know how to find the information you seek?

Can you set reminders that actually alert you to do something?

Most importantly, is your network impressed with your follow-up skills? After all, that is the true test if your process is working.

How Many People Should You Know?

This number will vary based on what you do and, more important-ly, what you can do for others. Realize that the more people you know, the more opportunities you have to be of assistance. Each instance of you doing so allows you to gain assistance in what you seek. It's a great equation that always works in your favor. You help someone, and both they and the universe move in ways to help you (see sections on "Law of Reciprocity" and "Law of Gen-erosity".

Don't be the person collecting contacts for the sake of collect-ing. Do so for the sake of helping more people. Each new person brings a chance at a new opportunity. Each new opportunity will likely lead to new connections and even more opportunities. The key is listening and asking good questions.

Be Connected
You Won't Know Who I Know Until I Get to Know You

As a connector, people often ask me to make introductions for them. As a rule, I am generally willing to make them. I always want to find out about you, what you want, and why you want it. If the answers seem genuine and logical, I will introduce you.

It's interesting how little I am able to do this for others. Not because I don't know the people they seek, but because a lot of people don't really know who they want to meet. But you're different. You already read the piece on knowing your targets.

I think people believe the idea popularized by Bob Burg "All things being equal, people do business with people they know, like and trust." Since that's true, how do you shorten the time to get known, liked and trusted?

1. Get introduced by mutual and trusted associates. This allows you to "borrow" the credibility of someone they (hopefully) know, like and trust already (don't screw this up).

2. Use the questions discussed in the section on "Common Ground." Common ground is the basis of all relationships so this practice helps build relationships fast!

3. Demonstrate integrity in your words and actions. People love working with people who are positive, don't speak ill of others and do what they said they will do.

4. Help them find what they seek. Helping someone is

66

a great way to ingratiate yourself to them.

Who Owns Your Network?

If you are in business development for anyone other than yourself, the question of who owns your network may come up. It's important to consider that you could spend vast amounts of time building your network so you can build someone else's business.

Here's the rub: they pay you to build their business. While I would suggest that networking is beneficial for far more than simply business growth, many people don't see it as such. If your boss is one of those people, they are going to see your network as something they paid you to build. The logic being that they pay you to grow business and networking is a means to that end.

It makes some sense. Consider the number of their clients, vendors, and prospects you will likely add to your network. Should you be able to work with them if a separation occurs? Think about the non-competes so many companies have their employees sign. Granted, most are relatively unenforceable, especially in right-to- work states. How does "your" network fit into this space?

So adding people related to their business to your network may be a cause for trouble. What about the network you had in place before? You know the one that likely helped you find the job in the first place?

Do we have to take snapshots of our network every time we take on a new role? Is our network negotiable? How much gray surrounds this topic? And who will color it up for us?

While Networking Standardization doesn't exist, common sense does. Each of us has to consider this and decide how to value and use our networks. This will be a conversation you'll want to have during the interview process.

I remember working for a telecom company back in 2000. As a sales jock in telecom your job was basically to wear out the leather on your shoes and "pull" as many doors as you could in a day (walk into offices uninvited...the dreaded cold call). The goal was to grab 50 new cards a day. That's quite a collection after 2-3 months (tenure of the average rep). They (sales management) didn't want you taking those cards when you left either. They were "property" of the company since they paid you for the time you used to collect them. Man did the vultures come out the day a person left. Everyone wanted to go through those cards to see if there was any unsifted gold in there. Strange, eh?

But if the company "owns" the card you collect while cold calling, should they own the network you build too? I really don't think so, but it's not really up to me.

10 Things I Want Networkers To Know

1. It's about you, it's about me, and it's about our network, in that order.

2. Givers do gain. And giving others an opportunity to help you is still giving.

3. Networking can and should happen anywhere, all the time.

4. Go to networking events to network, not to sell.

5. If you are not meeting people, understanding their needs, and connecting them with the resources to see them fulfilled, *and if the same isn't happening for you*, you are not networking.

6. Curiosity, great listening skills, and an interest in others' success are the keys to being an effective net-worker.

7. Your best networking partners are usually the people you might think are your competition.

8. It's not what you know, who you know, or who knows you, it's all about how you're known.

9. Being interested makes you far more interesting than trying to be interesting.

10. Networking is an investment that takes time and yields significant returns.

12 tips to make you a better networker

Show up-   This is first and will always be. If you don't show up ready to network both online and off, you won't be effective at it. Networking takes effort...hence the word "working". Take the time to understand how the following ideas fit into your networking world, and you will do well.

Know what you have to offer-   Without a solid understanding of what you have to offer, you will find it much harder to give. How often do you give any of the following to your network: Time, Energy, Attention, Money, Expertise, Connections or Resources? **See, you have a lot more to give than you thought.**

Know what you want to receive- When it comes to networking most people want the same thing: More Business. That's great! But unless you can tell us what kind of business will be best for you, we will have a hard time giving it to you. The more specific your ASK, the better. **People want to help you, but we can't do so unless you tell us how.**

Consider "After You" Networking- Everyone worries about making a great first impression. Use this to your advantage. When meeting someone new, let them go first. Several benefits are yours with this approach: A. **You'll demonstrate your desire to be interested prior to being interesting.** B. You'll have a solid understanding of who they are and what they need. C. They'll be able to actually listen to you when it's your turn to speak. D. If they don't listen to you, you know exactly what kind of person they are.

Use online networking effectively- So many tools, so little time. The good news is they can help you expand your network FAST. **The most important thing about online networking is creating and maintaining relationships**. The power of "search" is one you must understand. It's about finding the folks you need while making sure those who need you can easily find you too.

Give when you can- You already have an idea of what you have to offer, be sure to give it when you can. We have all heard the phrase "Giver's gain" made popular by Dr. Ivan Misner of BNI fame. It's time to put it to good use. Give. Give a lot. Give every chance you can. **I firmly believe that giving others a clear path (ASK) on how they can help you is an act of giving.**

Connect others-   **Networking is about levering the relationships you have to create the relationships you need.** This requires introductions. Don't sit and wait for others to introduce you.
Make connections for them too. The more proactive you can be in
this space, the better.

Know why networking works-   Networking works when people
work at it. If you give to me, I'm going to make sure I do my best to
give to you…This is the Law of Reciprocity. Similarly if you give to
me, I'm going to make sure I pay it forward and give to someone
else. This is the Law of Generosity. Universal Laws **dictate much
of our life and networking is no different.**

Ask. Listen. Repeat.-   When it comes to networking, and all
good communications for that matter, Asking good questions
and listening to the answers is at the heart of it all. Make sure you
practice these important skills again and again. **If you've ever
wanted to honor someone, ask them questions about their
favorite topic (themselves) and actually take time to listen to
the answer.**

Make it easy for others to help you-   It's a big world and you've
got a lot to do. You'll do far more with the assistance of others. **Don't make others chase YOU to help YOU.** Make your
contact information easy to access by putting it on your e-mail
signature and social media profiles. When someone does say they
will help, call or e-mail them. Don't make them reach out to you.

Say thank you-   It's important to update your network on the
status of any referral they have given you. It's vital that you thank
them for it. You can make a phone call and say thanks just slightly
easier than you can go by a gift card to their favorite store or
restaurant. **Just be sure to let them know they and their faith in
you are appreciated.**

Follow up-   This is the number one area where sales people and networkers blow big opportunities...they fail to follow up. Following up is so crucial that I dedicated the entire last chapter of my book to it. **You can follow up by letter, e-mail, telephone, video chat, social media or several other ways.** How you do it isn't nearly as important as you actually doing it.

Thank you for taking the time to read these. Proper implementation of these ideas will result in big praise from both your wallet and your network.

We have spent considerable time looking at the things one must know before they can really network effectively. Now it's time to look at applying some skill at an actual event. The third section of the book is called:

Connecting at a
Networking Event

It's so easy to spot the people at an event who get it and even easier to spot those who don't. Let's start with this very simple, yet important concept.

You Go to Networking Events to Network, Not to Sell

I am not a big fan of pet peeves, but if I had one it would be the people at networking events who try to cram their product or service down my throat. I am not there for you to sell me stuff. You shouldn't be there if you need to sell stuff right now. That's not how it works.

My good friend Charlie likens networking to farming and construction. Unlike the hunting mentality in sales, networking takes time. You actually have to develop relationships. Those things just don't happen overnight. Sure, many of us were at the right place, in the right time, where we happened to meet the right person, and said the right thing to them. And that led to a sale almost on the spot. Trust me, this just doesn't happen all that often. Think of it like a cold call close. You do remember the cold call close, right?

A "cold call close" is when you call on a client (either in person or on the telephone), absolutely out of the blue, and sell them your product or service. Even in businesses where this practice actually occurs (like in telecom service sales) it doesn't happen often.

Most of us aren't going to sell something just walking down the street. Sales don't often happen at networking events either and nor should they. So stop trying. *Please.* (This gives me an idea...maybe instead of hosting networking events I'll start hosting "sales" events. Ha!)

Instead, try going to an event with the stated goal of meeting some people you can help grow in their business and who may be able to help you do the same.

Most salespeople who have to cold call as part of their business development process know that they are better served trying to gather information on the cold call and trying to set an appointment, rather than making a sale. Why would meeting someone at a networking event be any different?

Think about it, you are at a networking event meeting people with whom you could do business (for the first time.) Why would you expect those interactions to be any different than a cold call? They are exactly the same scenario, with the exception that the person you just met is there to network with you.

So let them. Be easy to network with. Do the same thing you would do on any other cold call. Gather information to see if you can help them. But this time try helping them in two ways and use the third approach to help you.

1. Can you provide contacts and/or information that can help them and their business grow?

2. Can someone in your network do the same for them?

3. Do they seem like they may be able to help you and your business?

Make sure to look for ways you can be of service first and if you find that you can ask for the appointment.

High on the list of things Networking Events aren't...

It's Not a Race to Collect Cards

I am not sure why so many people look at networking events like it is a game to be won or a contest to be had. The number one thing some people try to do is see how many cards they can give or get. What a total waste. Do you have any idea what happens with "all" of those cards that they are quickly passing out?? They are even more quickly being erased from the minds of people who receive them.

Some People are observant. They pay attention to you and your actions. They want to connect with like-minded folks who may be able to help them and their business at some point. When you are in full "Card Dissemination" mode, it's obvious what you are do-ing. At least it is to them. You are turning them off. People don't see what value you can create for them. They only see what value you are TRYING to create for yourself. Networking is about relation-ships. Handing out unwanted cards at events DOES NOT equate to creating relationships.

I rarely hand out cards at events. Not because I don't want people to connect with me. Heck, I am one of the easiest people to find there are.[8] I don't hand out cards because for the people I want to contact, I will get their cards and contact them. When you have their contact info, you control the follow up. We will learn more about that in the last section of the book.

There are lots of folks who collect cards like it's their job. And to an extent it is, but not at the rate they're doing it. What's worse is that many people end up doing nothing with these cards.

Is it because they have too many cards? Is it because they have no reason to follow up? Is it because they're too busy? It's hard to say, but it could be a combination of all of those things. Maybe it's because their goals at a networking event are off. The reality is, if you walk out of a meeting with five good connections, you are far better off than having 50 new cards.

Why, because most of those 50 people will have zero idea who you are when you contact them later. People are there to meet and connect with others, not just get cards. That should be your purpose in going too. Even those folks, who gather cards for the purpose of increasing the numbers in their database, may be surprised to find out how quickly their newsletters or other offers end up in the trash of those who don't know them. Relationship building takes time. Deal with it.

We've all met someone like the following. Please, *please*

read this.

You Don't Want To Be That Guy

You have seen them. We all have. If you don't recognize the following description, I implore you, look in the mirror. If you find that I am describing you, I respectfully request that you make some changes. At the very least, please don't attend the same events I do.

The individual I am describing is the one who comes up to you, with a fake smile, and his business card in the hand he intends to shake yours with. He doesn't want to learn about you, just to add you to his database, he could care less about anything having to do with you, your business or your needs…

You see, somewhere along the way, he learned that he who has the most contacts wins. While that could be the case, last I checked, there was no such prize, and networking isn't a game. It's a way to help others, and hopefully yourself, along the way.

So, you and "that guy" are engaged in conversation and you find yourself wondering if you are in fact talking to that guy. Here are some identifying factors you should be able to recognize:

1. They tell you all about themselves and their business without asking a question of you or being invited to do so. Just when you think it's your turn to speak, *poof*, they're off to talk to someone else.

2. They spend the duration of your conversation (or should we call it a monologue?) looking around the room to see who else is there. They certainly don't want to speak with you if there may be someone better to meet.

3. They demonstrate poor listening skills. Let's assume you're actually granted the opportunity to speak, you will likely be interrupted or just feel that you aren't really being heard.

4. The individual has a bad case of one-up-man-ship. You know the drill, anytime you say something, this individual relates a story to what you said, that in his mind, was way cooler than what you did.

5. They tell you about their cool newsletter and that they will be sending you one.

6 . They name drop so that you will be impressed with all of the cool people they know.

The real problem with that guy is that most people feel the same way about him. So when it comes to leveraging the relationships he has, you quickly realize that he has very little... both leverage and relationships.

There are lots of people you can be at a networking event, that guy is not one of them.

Now that you have some ideas about what not to do, let's take a look at the things that should be on your "To Do" list.

Good Wingmen Wanted

My first rule of networking is very simple: SHOW UP!

For some reason, that is awfully difficult for many people to grasp.

The idea of bringing a wingman should make this easier. For the few of you who aren't familiar with the concept of a wingman, I offer this: Your wingman is the person who you agree to ride or simply arrive with at a networking event (or bar for you single folk). Consider them your accountability partner and your potential for fun.

A good wingman makes sure you get there. This happens for two reasons:

1. You feel accountable to them because you know

they are going to make it and you don't want to be the one who committed but doesn't show up.

2. They will bust your chops if you don't show up.

So the wingman needs to be someone for whom you have some respect. If you don't have that, make a wager. If one of you doesn't show, you owe the other lunch, drinks, or cash. Whatever works for the two of you.

Here's the key about the wingman, they are there to get you there, not to stand by your side for the whole event. It always boggles my mind when I see two people from the same company talking to one another at a networking event. News flash: you couldn't sell them anything at the office, do you think they are going to help you be a better networker?

If you spend more than 10% of your time talking only to your wingman, you messed up. I should point out that by no means does your wingman have to be from your company. In fact, it is better if they aren't. Ideally, they would be one of your target referral partners. This way each person you meet could be of benefit to you both.

Ideally, you can double your networking efforts and introduce each other to new folks. Make sure you communicate who it is that each of you are looking to meet. **By doubling the amount of people looking for your ideal contact, you just doubled the likelihood of finding them.** The same is true for your wingman. Working together will yield greater results quicker than working apart. Be sure you two do your planning in advance of the event. You will also want to set aside time to debrief after.

It's okay to share a quick story or laugh together, but what you really want to be sharing is your new contacts. You can't make those by talking to each other. Split up. Go meet new people. Share the successes.

Great, you made it to the event, what's next?

The One Accessory You Need To Wear At Every Networking Event

You can see it from across the room. When worn correctly, it makes you ten times more approachable. It's like a magnet that attracts great people to you. It comes in many different shapes, sizes, and even colors. Regardless or your age, gender, body-type, or level of affluence, there is certain to be one that fits you perfectly. It complements every outfit and never clashes with your bag or brown shoes.

Have I mentioned that it's free? How about the fact that you already have one?

Have you guessed what it is? Your smile.

Your smile, your genuine smile, will make people come to you. People are naturally attracted to those they perceive as happy. A smile is the finest indicator of happiness. If you look like you are enjoying yourself, others will want to join in on the fun. Let them. You never know who your smile will attract.

Fun is contagious. And people want to be a part of a group that is having a good time.

Next time you're out at an event grab someone who you can laugh with. Purposefully sit away from others and laugh it up. If it is genuine and you look like you're having a good time, within moments someone else will join you. If the three of you are having fun, a larger group will continue to gather. It's a fun experiment that proves how others love to be around those of us who are having a good time.

Use your smile as the attraction tool that it is.

For What To ASK

Obviously I can't tell you that, but I should be able to point you in the right direction.

It's very important to give people the opportunity to help you. This is what networking is about, assuming that you are helping them too. From a spiritual perspective, step 1 is always ASK. You will not be properly provided for, if you don't first ask for what you seek.

If you don't feel that you have everything you want right now, there are only a handful of reasons that could be.

1. You're not in alignment with or clear on what you seek.

2. You don't believe you are entitled to what you want.

3. You don't follow the signs that are presented to you that point you in the direction you need to go.

4. Your asks are not being properly received.

This particular section is going to focus on issue one. The other

81

three will get their due attention, don't worry. ;-)

Let me explain what I mean by "not being in alignment with what you seek." So often I talk with people that tell me they want to make more money. I am not knocking that as a goal by any stretch of the imagination. BUT, saying you want more money and doing ABSOLUTELY NOTHING to get it, suggests that your intentions and your actions are out of alignment. When your intentions are clear and your actions support them, you are in alignment.

Other reasons people may not be in alignment is because they are seeking things that aren't good for their Being.

Let's look at getting clear on what you seek. Aside from more money, do you know what it is that you want? This isn't always an easy process. It requires a lot of thought and the ability to get very quiet with ourselves. So many of us think that the answers to the questions we have are outside of us. Not the case. Everything you seek to know is and has been inside of you. So my suggestion to you is ask yourself some questions and then get really, really quiet so that you may hear the answers. The questions to help you grow your business could look like this:

- What does my ideal client look like?

- Who refers me the most business?

- What types of companies make good strategic partners for me?

- If I could work with only three companies, who would they be?

82

Those questions are all good, but what if you already know you are not in the right *role*? You need to start with a different set of questions:

- If I could be anything in this life, what would I be?

- Where do my talents intersect with the needs of the world?

- What do I really enjoy doing that can earn me a good living?

- What are my strengths?

In simplest terms, ask yourself what would make you wildly happy (either in business growth or career direction) and chart a course toward it. When you figure out what it is that is going to bring you bliss, you have just uncovered for what you should ask.

You're there, you're smiling, you know what you're asking for and you're ready to meet people...

How to Work a Room

If you're like most people, you walk into a networking event and are instantly overwhelmed. And that's okay. There is a lot going on. There are lots of people conversing. Many of whom look like they've known each other for a long time. A good networking event has lots of hands to shake and opportunities to be discovered. How will you make it through? How will you find the people, in this vast sea of faces that make sense for you to meet?

Hopefully you have read the sections on your ideal clients and partners. If not, we'll wait. Seriously, if you don't know who your ideal targets are, how can you expect anyone to help you find them? Go read them...we're waiting.

Okay, so you now know who you need to meet. Now you have to find them. In the meantime, you will likely be glad- handing with some folks who aren't on your list. Here are some rules for that:

1. The person with whom you are speaking needs to feel like the most important person in the room. This has to happen even if you end up sacrificing the opportunity to meet the next person. It's okay, you won't be with them long. Pay excellent attention to them.

2. Set a time limit for each "non–essential" conversation. It should be under seven minutes depending on how long the event is and how many people are on your target list. If you have reason to speak with them for longer, you need to ask for their card and setup a follow-up conversation. Remember, they are there to network too. Do both of you a favor and schedule that meeting on the spot. Most people keep their calendar in their phone so no excuses.

3. Qualify what an essential conversation is. You will likely meet quite a few people at the event. Only a select few will be the essential ones on your list. Know what that list looks like. This is something that you will need to have an idea of in advance of the event. But do yourself a favor and don't make hard, fast rules here. Allow for the magic of serendipity.

4. You don't know who anyone knows until you get to know them. Don't make the assumption that the person with whom you are speaking is of no use to you.

5. Have three different "ASKS" at the ready. This approach, when very specifically applied, allows for multiple opportunities to come your way.

6. If you have the opportunity to introduce two colleagues, do it. This is a very powerful thing to do in terms of creating relationship capital. When these two people meet, they will have but one thing immediately in common, you. What do you think will be their topic of conversation? That's right, you! Be the catalyst for good things happening for others and good things will happen for you.

7. You have business cards for a reason, but do you know what that reason is? If you are "that guy" and run around inside the event sticking your cards in as many hands as will take it, your cards will all likely end up in the same place...the circular file, the deep six, the bottomless pit, the trash. Only use your cards for one of two reasons:

   a. To get someone else's card. It's like a trade of sorts. Ask the question: "Care to exchange cards?" or "Mind if I give you one of these (said holding your card) for one of those (pointing at theirs)?"

   b. To take down notes from the conversation that you WILL use during your follow up. Please note that there are groups of business professionals (Japanese come immediately to mind) who find the practice of writing on cards HIGHLY offensive. It is very important to know your audience. Understand cultural differences.

8. It's okay to spend some time with people you already know. Yes you are there to create new relationships, but you also need to strengthen the ones you have. Rule of thumb: spend less than 40% of your time with people you already know. Quick caveat: if you are with a prospect who is very close to closing, do your best to introduce him to their potential clients and/or your centers of influence. This is a great way for you to add value to them that they will likely appreciate. And hopefully it allows you to separate yourself from the competition.

9. Always have an escape plan. Invariably, you will end up speaking with someone who is a waste of your time. You need to avoid that at all costs. Let's face it, sometimes seven minutes is a really long time. Don't panic, I got your back. You have options and none of them involve "toughing it out." You will learn how to gracefully exit a conversation a little later in this section.

So you've buzzed around the room a couple of times, but you haven't found your targets...

Finding the People with Whom You Need to Speak

If you are going to be at a networking event, you better know with whom you intend to spend time. As much fun as it is to go to these events and talk to folks you already know, that isn't your purpose. After all, you went to be a networker, not a social butterfly, right? So here are three tips that will help you maximize your time at an event.

1. Check the list of attendees.

Sometimes you will be able to see who is there long before the event happens. If at all possible, check this list and find the types of people you need to meet. Strategically plan your time.

Ideally you will spend 7-10 minutes with each of these people getting to know them. If there is one hour allocated for networking, realize that you will only get to speak to 4-8 people on your list. Just because you are looking to speak with them, they may not be looking to speak with you. In fact, they will likely already be engaged in a conversation when you find them. Allowing them time to finish that conversation, will likely throw you off of your schedule. And that's okay.

There will also be times when the list of attendees is only available at the event itself. Not to worry. You know how to read the list and find the type of people you seek.

Quickly scan the list, make note of those few you want to meet, and go meet them. Pretty simple.

Ahh, but what to do when no lists exist? This is where you need to be a little creative. There are a couple of people you should target if you find yourself in this predicament...

2. Meet the host.

Why? Because they are most likely the one who would have created the list that you didn't get. They likely know the most people in the room. It should become your task to go speak with them, tell them the types of people you wish to meet and see if they would be kind enough to make an introduction or two. Realize that they are likely to be very busy with heir hosting duties. If they can't introduce you personally, make sure that you ask if it's okay that you use their name. That way you can say to your new contact "I was speaking with *host's name* and they told me you were someone I had to meet."

3. Find the connector.

So we agree that the host will be busy. Heck, they may not even be in the same spot long enough for you to track them down. The next person you should look to befriend is the one with the largest gathering around them. In most instances, these folks are the connectors in the room; the ones that know a lot of people and a lot of people know them. Utilize the same approach that you would use with the host and ask them for their help. It's amazing how willing people are to oblige if you simply and specifically ask for help.

Following these simple tips should help you get connected to the people you want to meet in a much more efficient manner. And, if you can connect with the exact people you need to meet quickly, you just made way better use of your networking time.

There's an art to "interrupting" people at a networking meeting.

How To Enter Into A Conversation

Great news, you've spotted them. The one person you need to talk with to make this event a total success. Bad news, they're engaged in a conversation. You walk closer. You hear the conversation. It sounds like a good one. You don't want to be rude, but you certainly can't let this important opportunity pass you by. What to do?

Sure you can stand idly by and wait until the conversation ends, but what if another one picks up before you get your shot?

Alternatively you could rush into the middle of the conversation, politely excuse yourself by saying "this is the one person I came to meet."

Both may be effective or be a total failure.

Try this. Walk right up to the two, three, or however many are gathered and pause like you are awaiting entrance into the "circle of conversation." One of two things will occur almost instantly:

A. They will stop speaking, look at you, and mention that they are having a private conversation. This is rarely the case at a networking event. On the off chance it does happen, thank them for the acknowledgement, and let the person with whom you intend to speak know that you would like to chat with them. Perhaps mention how long you will be at the event. Then leave them to their conversation.

The more likely scenario is:

B. They will side step and allow you into the conversation. Here you will have a choice to make. Do you change the conversation or do you flow with it? I almost always opt for the latter (time constraints or lack of knowledge would be the only items to deter me). There will be a natural time for you to introduce yourself. Be patient.

This approach takes some getting used to and is highly effective. You definitely want to get an idea of what they are discussing before you walk (or talk) into it. That way you can be assured to add some value.

At most networking events, you will see the people you spoke with earlier. Look like a pro by calling them by name, even if it's only an hour later.

Remembering The People You Just Met

One of everyone's favorite words to hear is their own name. When you are meeting someone for the first time, you can make that meeting more memorable for both of you by sprinkling their name throughout the conversation. They'll enjoy it because you keep uttering their favorite sound. You will enjoy it because it improves your memory of them and your meeting.

Saying their name is important, but if you really want to solidify the connection in your brain, also make an association.

When looking at the person, can you make an association about their physical appearance? My friend Barry Demp presents on "The Do's and Don'ts of Networking" and talks about name associations. Barry is balding so he associates the name Barry with the word Bald. It certainly works.

Greg Wolf uses the catch phrase "The only wolf you want at your door." It's certainly nice when people give you the associations so you don't have to think about them, but what if you don't have that luxury? Tie their most obvious feature tot their name. If they have curly hair and their name is Carol, it's pretty easy. If they have a large curved nose and their name is Peter, maybe you can think-Okay Peter has a hooked nose. Peter Pan had Captain Hook. This guy has a Captain Hook nose from Peter Pan. Captain Hook Nose= Peter. You get it.

Sometimes tying it to their clothes is easier to do. No one will ever forget the knot hat Aretha Franklin wore to sing at President Obama's first inauguration. Sure you can pull the letters for "hat" out of her name, but it's just as easy to remember ugly hat[9] Aretha. Just don't depend on her wearing the same hat the next time you see her.

Here is the #1, most important secret to remembering people's names: LISTEN to them when they tell you. **You can't remember something you never knew.** (Most people think they have a memory problem…they don't. They have a listening problem). We are so busy conjuring up some great story or some good response when others are speaking that we don't ever really hear their name in the beginning. That is the key. We have to hear it AND be listening the first time they say it. Don't worry about what you are about to say to impress them. If you are listening, the right words will fall out of your mouth when needed.

You may also write down some notes on their business card. Rewriting their name will also help. Turns out Bill Clinton used to carry a note book and write the names of the people he just met in it. (I wonder what was written next to Monica's name.) The more notes you have, the more likely you are to remember the conversation, and more importantly be able to tell them a story so that they will remember you too.

Nametags, Handshakes, And Look 'Em In The Eye… Oh My!

Earlier I shared some ways to remember people's names. Want to know the best one of all time? Look at their nametag. It's easy, right? Well not all events have them, but if you're at one that does, use it.

Here's the important thing about nametags, most people put them on the wrong side, which is the opposite of the *Right* side. That's correct. Your nametag should be worn on the right side of your chest. Why? Because when you go to shake hands with someone, you shake with your right hand. That hand extends toward the person you're meeting. As your hand moves toward them, so does your

91

nametag. When you put it on the left side, it becomes harder to see.

Speaking (well, writing) of handshakes, they sure do tell people a lot about you. Some people squeeze too tightly. Others feel like a limp noodle. Some people pump your hand until it feels like it's going to fall off. Every once in a while you find the perfect (and hard to believe) right "Pump to Grip" blend. Then you run into a whole different set of challenges.

People think if you come from the top and push their hand down, you're trying to be dominant. If you come from the bottom to meet theirs, you're submissive. You don't need to turn their hand, pull them toward you, or push them away.

Simple rule for handshakes: line up the space where your thumb and first finger make an L (on your right hand) with the same space on their hand. Once those two spaces are connected, wrap your four fingers around the whole of their hand. Apply enough pressure that they feel it, but not so much as to bend their fingers. Nobody likes a "dead fish," or even worse, the "Bone crusher." From your elbow, pump the handshake twice. It should travel less than 8 inches up and down. You don't want to be that over- exaggerator in the world of pumping either.

There is only one more thing to tell you about handshakes, and it doesn't even involve hands.

We really do judge people based on their ability to look us in the eye. When you shake someone's hand for the first time make sure you meet their gaze. It also helps to have that little sparkle that comes to your eyes when you smile. Try it, it really is infectious.

For more valuable information on these topics google: "5 steps to building better business relationships faster" and enjoy the video.

We talked earlier about the ways to enter a conversation, the opposite skill is every bit as necessary.

Exiting A Conversation

We can't be all things to all people and neither can people be all things for us. It's just the way the world works. Occasionally, as you are in your networking circles, you will meet some people who just aren't your "cup of tea." This could be for any number of reasons:

- You find them brash.

- There really isn't any common ground between the two of you.

- They work for a company that you have a bad history with. Your personality types are remarkably different.

- And the list goes on.

For whatever reason, you two just don't click. As such, you will find it prudent to leave the conversation. The reality is you have a fixed amount of time at a networking event, so there is no sense wasting it talking to a dud. Here's the tricky part; how do you leave the conversation gracefully?

You'll notice that I use the word "gracefully." Why? Because there are lots of ways to do it ungracefully:

You can say you have to use the restroom and make a dash (by the way, this could be a true story.)

Maybe it's time to refill your drink?

Perhaps you want to use the "look at your watch and it's time to go line."

Here's the deal with any of these, if you pull it, you need to do it. *Immediately.*

While all of these have the desired effect, that is LEAVING the conversation, they're not the best way to do it. Here are two examples that the pros use:

1. If you're at the right event, you are bound to see someone you MUST speak with. Locate that person and then point them out to your current conversation partner. Explain that you have been trying to speak with them for X amount of time or just why you need to speak with them. Get their buy in about how important this conversation will be to you. Thank them for their time and make a bee line for this next person.

2. This is the best way. Introduce them to someone who you think they should meet. If you did a good job of asking them the right questions and listening to them in the beginning, you will know who they need to meet. If you are aware of the people in the room, you will likely know at least one person who they should be talking to. Make that introduction. It's quick, easy, and if done right, both people will be happy you did it.

Here is a key point to remember: Just because you didn't enjoy a conversation with someone doesn't mean that others won't.

In order to be successful you need the right tools. In networking, two of the right tools are your ability to ask the right questions and listen.

The Most Powerful Networking Question Ever

I first heard this question when I was listening to Bob Burg speak on Networking, back in Northeast Ohio, in 1998. I have since also read it in his book "Endless Referrals" and used it numerous times. It has also been the feature of numerous conversations on discussion site http://www.myvirtualpowerforum.com, which is now http://brandergy.com (a great place to discuss and learn about online networking).

When I tell you it is a powerful question, I mean that it is one that gets results. What results? I am glad you asked.

1. It tells your conversation partner that you are definitely interested in them and what they have to say.

2. It gets to the heart of the matter.

3. 90% of the time, when I have used it at a networking event, I have been able to make valuable introductions almost immediately.

Allow me to elaborate on #3. When I have asked this powerful question in the past, and really listened to the answer, it sets this amazing process in motion. That process is that one of the next 4 or 5 people I talk with, is the exact person the individual, I just asked that question, said they wanted to meet. Here's the thing, I don't ask it all the time. Why? Because 1. I don't want to wear out the magic. 2. There are other good questions that can be asked as well.

You're probably wondering what this awesome question is. Here it goes:

How would I recognize if someone I am speaking with is a good referral for you?

I did learn of a shorter version while reading a book called "Networking Fuel" by Michael Waite. The book was okay, but just the question "Who Needs to Know You?" was well worth the time I spent reading it.

Use this question to make the following happen.

Get Two People to Talk About You

When you introduce two people for the first time, they are likely to find things they have in common. Since you are the one thing they both know, you are bound to become a part of that conversation. If the introduction was a good one, they will be saying good things about you.

This is important for a couple of reasons:

1. Part of their discussion is likely to involve how they can help you. Hopefully, you have done a good job with communicating your ask to at least one of them. Having two people brainstorming on your behalf can be highly beneficial. As they converse, they will spark ideas that should serve your business well. The better the connection you have made, the more likely they will be to actually act on their discussion and help you out.

2. Having people speak well of you creates good juju for you. Let's assume that they aren't able to uncover a good opportunity for you. The universe still can. That good juju goes out and has to find a way to come back to you. It can be as simple as walking out to your parked car, standing at the meter that expired an hour ago, and not having a ticket. It could also be getting a call, from that client you have been pursuing for months, telling you they are ready to sign that purchase order.

Either scenario is certainly in your favor.

Good things happen to folks who make good connections. Who can you connect today?

Every good book should have a top 10 list or two. Here's one on what networking events are not.

What Networking Events Aren't

10. They aren't a good place to try out your fancy new cologne.

9. They aren't the right place for you to worry about

"being seen."

8. They aren't in existence for you to practice one-up-man-ship.

7. They aren't the place for you to drone on about all of the problems you have in your business.

6. They aren't the repository for you to unload all of your freshly printed materials.

5. They aren't the opportunity for you to badmouth your competition or anything else for that matter.

4. They aren't the forum for you to repeatedly practice your entire 10 minute sales pitch, repeatedly.

3. They aren't the place for you to go and only speak with folks you already know.

2. They aren't the arena for you to be interesting before being interested.

1. They aren't the event where you will ever win a prize for most business cards collected.

To close this section on "You at a networking event," I want you to consider the following:

Ways to Be Memorable, they're not all good

It's a heck of a lot easier to start a conversation with someone, after a networking event, when they remember you. Here's the rub, so many of us don't engage in memorable or meaningful conversation. Worse than that, there are those of us who are remembered, but for the wrong thing.

Here is a quick list of some ways to be remembered at a networking event:

Note that I said they are not all good!

1. The most important networking accessory you can wear is very simple: It's a smile. People like to be around people who look like they're having fun and feel good about themselves.

2. The person to whom you are speaking is the most important person in the room. Honor them. Listen to them. Ask them questions. These are the ways they will know that they are important to you.

3. If you want to be remembered as a great conversationalist, let the person with whom you are speaking talk about themselves. It's amazing, how they can talk for 17 out of 20 minutes and walk away thinking you are a dynamic and interesting conversationalist.

4. Ask how you can be of assistance and be genuinely interested in the answer. You are there (or at least

should be) to help. Do so. Networking starts with an expressed need. Let them express their needs and do what you can to see those needs fulfilled.

5. Be a connector. People will tell you how you can help them. Do so. It's very powerful to have someone call you to thank you for the outstanding referral or opportunity that was generated as a result of your interaction with them.

On to the flip side

1. Be rude. Interrupt often. Stare at your phone as they speak.

2. Talk only about you and your needs. Pay no mind to what they have to say or what may be important to them.

3. Look around the room constantly, as if there may be someone better there for you to be speaking to.

4. Play the one-up-man-ship game. Every time they tell you a story, or something of interest, let them know that your story is way better or more important.

Needless to say these are all ways to be memorable. The difference is one set of ideas will get you a lot farther than the other set. Choose wisely.

Now that you have some ideas on how to network effectively face to face, let's look at the equally huge networking opportunity available in the comfort of your pajamas. ;-)

You Connecting Online

12 tips to make your online networking time more effective

This was written in 09 and is every bit as germane today. What would you add to it?

1. Have a plan. Understand what you want to get out of your online networking time and what you have to give to it.

2. Upload your address book. This step will allow you to grow your networks faster. **Larger networks lead to more opportunities.**

3. Realize the importance of being interested over being interesting. Networking isn't only about what's in it for you. **It's about what I can do for you, what you can do for me and what we can do together.**

4. Ask good questions. Social networking is really all about conversations. One of the best ways to engage others in conversation is to ask questions.

5. Be interested in helping others. **Without a healthy interest in the well being of others, any networking will be a total waste of your time.**

6. Make connections. Know two people that need to meet? Introduce them. Networking sites like Linkedin, Twitter and Facebook make this very easy to do.

7. Shine the light on others. **By helping to spread the word of others you actually help spread your own word as well.**

8. **Spend time working your online network daily.** It doesn't have to be all day, and it shouldn't be overwhelming. But you do need to make a consistent effort on this.

9. Alter the time you are online. Most people are creatures of habit and are online at the same time everyday. If you want maximum exposure, mix up the times so different people are seeing your message.

10. Upload a photo. People do business with people. **Having a photo online makes you human, accessible and more interesting.** This is true regardless of how bad you think the photo is.

11. Find another medium by which to connect- Can you meet them in person? Do so. If not, pick up the phone. **It's great to connect online over keystrokes, but it's also important to do voice to voice or face to face networking.**

12. Get started. There isn't a reason you can conceive that would exonerate you from doing this. Online networking is the most important thing to hit the

internet thus far. If you need help, call me!

Great online sites

I am pretty sure that by the time you finish reading this section, a new online networking site will be born. It is all the rage. People are connecting online at a myriad of places, for a myriad of reasons.

There are business networking sites, friend networking sites, hobby networking sites, photo sharing sites, news aggregating sites, music downloading sites and even sites that are designed to help people cope with specific diseases. Effectively, if there is a cause or a way for people to establish common ground, there is a site for it.

Some of the most popular sites out there today include:

LinkedIn- this is currently the premiere business networking site. (www.linkedin.com). 95% business 5% fun.

Facebook- originally developed for college students, this is the most robust site for connecting with people in a multitude of ways. Facebook is moving more toward business, but still a lot about friends and family. 35% business 65% the rest.

Twitter- The fastest way to connect with what's new, what's now, and what's next. It's hard for a lot of people to "get it," but those that do, get a lot in return. (twitter.com)

Google+ - The social networking attempt by Google. As such it warrants your attention and with over 235 Million active users, it's getting some.

Plaxo- this was originally more of an online contact management tool, but they have added some great networking opportunities. (plaxo.com)

Groupsites and Ning- are both great sites that anyone can easily use to develop their own networking sites. (groupsites.com & ning.com)

YouTube- The premiere destination to upload and watch videos on the web. (youtube.com)

myspace- at one point this was *the* social networking site. It has since become more a niche site, catering to music and other forms of entertainment. (myspace.com)

Flickr- is a great site that allows people to connect and share photos. (www.flickr.com) Pinterest (www.pinterest.com) and Instagram (www.instagram.com) are playing in this space as well.

There are also social bookmarking sites like: **digg, stumbleupon** and **del.ic.io.us** that allow people to share interesting things they find whilst on the net. (digg.com / www.stumbleupon.com / delicious.com)

Finally there are blog sites like **blogger** or **wordpress** (www.blogger.com & wordpress.com)

How do you know which one of these to spend time on? Well that depends on a few things:

What are your goals with using this technology? Hopefully they're
aligned to meeting your target clients and business partners.
Who are you trying to reach? If you haven't read the section
about target clients and partners, now is a great time to do so.

Which sites are your competitors and your customers using? I
should add the word effectively here. It doesn't matter what sites
they're using if they're not finding value in how they use them.

Do yourself a favor and determine your strategy before investing
a lot of time, because you can lose yourself for hours (and hours
and hours) if you don't.

Managing the Time You Spend Online

I remember I basically lost three weeks of my life when I first got
on Twitter. It was so new, so interesting, and so full of links to other
great content. I just couldn't help myself. I talk about "best practices" a lot. Losing weeks on Twitter certainly isn't one of them. So
what are best practices in this case?

Online networking, like face to face networking, takes time and energy. Much to most people's chagrin, it isn't a "build it and they will
come" situation. More importantly, you have to be aware of what
you build.

When you first join a site you will need to invest some time setting it up. Most online sites want a picture, a bio, and some contact
info, at the very least.

Have a digital picture (or more) of you on your hard drive so you
can easily upload it. If you are setting up a professional site, have
a professional looking photo. It may also benefit you to have a

professional photo in front of your corporate logo. If a casual site, a casual photo is fine. Some sites allow you to put up as many photos as you would like (Check the site for their requirements).

The only caution I have here is that most sites don't tell you *who* is looking at them. When you are looking for a new job, client, or business partner, these people may be looking at your photos on these sites. Make sure you are posting photos you are comfortable with them seeing.

As far as bios go, some are short, like text messages, and others can be longer than your resume. When you know your purpose for online networking, and what sort of site you're on, you will know what sort of information to include. If you're not sure, take a look at other profiles. Get an idea from others like you. If that doesn't work, Google "profile examples" *followed by the name of the site that you are working on.* Lots of people blog on these topics for each site. You will get some good ideas.

On most sites, the setup can be the longest part. Well, that's true unless you are a curious sort. It is pretty easy to get lost looking at what others have shared. If your purpose is staying in touch with people, you're on task. If not, you need to set time limits.

First things first, tell us a little about you.

Create a Magnetic Profile

If you had a nickel for every time someone told you that you HAD to be on this great networking website, you probably wouldn't need any more business. It's amazing how many sites there are and that they all have one thing in common: they want YOU to fill out your profile or your bio.

Seriously, it has gotten to the point where I have one bio that reads: "If you found me here you have already read way too many of the bios I have written." For the record, I wrote that out of a bit of frustration and DO NOT recommend it as a best practice! ;-)

So how do we balance, the amount of time this practice takes, while showing some ROI (Return On Investment) on the time involved? For starters, make sure your profile "attracts" the type of viewers you want.

Let's look at LinkedIn as an example. LinkedIn allows you to effectively display your resume online. It asks you about your career and education history. It allows you to display your hobbies and interests and has a place for a summary.

Most people don't do a good job of filling this information out. I am not sure how it happens, but my guess is most people see all the requested information when they sign up and decide they will plug in a couple of key points (current company, title, and where they went to school/major) and decide they will do the rest later. Well, we all know when later comes...Oh, that's right. We have no idea when later comes.

Filling out your LinkedIn profile properly will take you 30 minutes or so. Deal with it. This could be the single best 30 minutes you spend this week or month. Not only does it give you the opportunity to reflect on your past accomplishments, it could bring you new opportunities in the future.

Write a catchy and accurate headline. This is a great place to grab our attention and quickly tell us what you do. It's important because when doing a search on these sites your title, name and location may be the only thing that shows up. If I do a search on LinkedIn for "marketing director in Detroit" you need to make sure your profile stands out above the 10 on the page. I like how twitter does profiles/bios. They give you 150 characters in which to do it. It's amazing how much info you can fit into that space when you are forced to do so.

Talk about "who you are."

Many of these sites have an area for a "summary." Most folks summarize their current work experience and consider this done. Sure that's a great way to check off the task, but does it really help the reader? No. Especially since there is an area for you to tell us about your job under "experience". This is the area where you want to engage the person by showing them who you are. What are your values? Share your thoughts on networking. Tell us about your family. Make this interesting and personal. It doesn't have to be long, but it would be great if it made us feel like we got to know you.

Tell us about "what you do."

This should be an easy one, right? Well, recognize that there are lots of people who do what you do. How will you make your profile stand out? You need to make sure you are using KEYWORDS. Keywords are the words that people use when "searching" online. If you are in the Mortgage business, keywords may include: real estate, REO, home purchase, buyer, seller, refinance, foreclosure, property, you get the idea.

An important point to consider: we need to make sure that we are using the keywords that our industry uses as well as the keywords our clients use. My friend Charlie is in the advertising/marketing business and they do a lot of "identity" design. He has yet to get a call for *identity design*, but he sure gets a lot of people calling because they need a new logo. ;-)

William Butler Yeats said it best, "think like a wise man, but communicate in the language of the people."

It's good to have "past life regressions."

Well, maybe they don't have to be full-on regressions, but it is good for people to get to know about your past life. Why? Because they may have been a part of it. You know I believe that "all business is relationship business." We have some really strong relationships with people we are no longer connected to. Think about that. If you ran into your favorite "cube buddy" from your first job, your favorite boss from 6 years ago, a college suite mate, or whomever, you would likely be able to pick right up on a good conversation. And what's really interesting is that some of these folks may be in a position to now do business with us or our business.

We have some amazingly strong ties in our past. It would be wise to make sure those folks can find us and possibly help us in our future. Fill out the previous experience portion. Some of these sites are "smart" enough to recommend you connect with people from days of yore. Take them up on that cool matching feature and let them help you build a better network.

Hobbies and interests are interesting.

If "all business is relationship business" and relationships are built fastest around commonality, do I need to write more?

Seriously, take the time to share your passions. You would be amazed at what comes from this simple act. It's a great conversation starter, it can open doors that weren't previously opened and you may just land your next gig because of it.

Having recommendations show up on your profile page is a great way for others to feel good about you. If you have earned them, feel great about asking for them. If there are people you would feel good about writing them for, do so. You never know, they may write one for you. I will cover this more in detail in a little bit.

The more information you put in your profiles the more common ground you will be able to establish with others. In fact sites like LinkedIn and Facebook use the info you put in about your work and school experience to connect you with others who were there too. Think about how much smaller the world has gotten for us all since the rise of social networking.

Your online profiles are where people go to find out about you in the NOW world. Whether you are meeting a new client, vendor, or potential employer, they are checking you out online. What impression will they get?

You have a lot of choices when it comes to networking online.

Choosing The Right Online Groups For You

So many groups. So little time. How the heck will you ever find the ones that are right for you?

It all starts with your purpose.

If you know who you want to meet, this question becomes significantly easier to answer. Couple that knowledge with knowing where they hang out online and you are practically there.

Sites like LinkedIn and Facebook have special sections called groups. This is where they pare the millions of users into specific, like minded interactions.

Groups form around a single idea, cause, or company. There are groups for rock bands just like there are groups for your college alumni. There are groups for associations like those that support architects, accountants, and attorneys. The software giant Oracle has an Oracle alumni group (I don't think these people graduated from there) for the former employees.

Why are groups important? Because the only people that join them have a specific reason to do so. They have an interest in that group and what it's about. If your product or service solves a need for a specific group or you can learn from the members of that group than you had better jump in.

Most groups are very easy to join. It's a matter of sending a request to the group administrator and they will decide whether or not to accept you. Some groups have very strict criteria as to who may join. When they do, they normally post that for all to see. Other groups are totally secret. Good luck finding those. There are a lot of groups that are open, but like I said earlier, know your purpose for joining. Without knowing that, your membership could be a waste of your time.

You're bound to come across people you need to meet, so let's look at the right ways to reach out to them.

Making Associates Online

The short answer is: you make new associates online in the same manner you do in the real world. You start by finding out about one another and determine if there is a reason to continue to do so. It's a lot like rocket science without all of the rocket or any of the science.

The long answer is, oddly enough, longer. You start by finding someone and viewing their profile. Obviously some profiles are filled out extremely well and others aren't. Glean what you can from what is written. Don't make the assumption that because their profile isn't properly filled out that they aren't worth knowing. Lots of great and busy people get online and are still planning on "later" to fill out their profile.

If you see something you like, send them a note that says: "I came across your profile on *x* platform and I really like what you wrote about *X*." (Copy their sentence and paste it right into your note.)[10] Tell them why that sentiment resonates with you and suggest a way to follow up via either phone or email.

Lots of people try to set up face to face meetings through LinkedIn or other sites. Color me old fashioned, but I think a first meeting, if not at an event, should be over the phone. This gives you a chance to explore the synergies and determine if a face to face is in order. The reality is everybody is busy. There is no sense in meeting with a lot of people, under the guise of "networking," if we will only be "netting" (that's networking without any of the good work that can come from it.)

Make sure you are using this valuable vehicle the right way.

Conversation starters

Do you have a hard time engaging others in conversation? If you do, it's likely even more apparent now with Facebook and Twitter, right? Here are a few of the BE attitudes from Charlie and my presentation that can help:

Be funny- The world loves a clown. If you hear a good joke, "borrow" it. Make humorous observations about everyday life. I heard this guy named Jerry something or other...turns out he made a mint doing that.

Be bold- Chris Matthews on Hardball doesn't get the big bucks because he's namby pamby...he dots you between the eyes with his opinions.

Be quotable- Can't think of anything original? Use someone else's quotes. We have a whole history full of them.

Be thought-provoking- Say something that gives folks pause and makes them go hmmm

Be helpful- Offer tips that will improve others experience.

Be interesting- Share relevant information that is topical to the day.

Be interested- Ask about them. "ME" is everyone's favorite topic

Be yourself- This last one is THEE most important. No sense in trying to be someone else because you'll "attract" the wrong type of people.

Using Status Updates Effectively

Status updates are simply the fastest, easiest way to let your network know what's going on. The challenge is that so many of us are posting things that neither serve us or our network!

Think about it, does anyone really care if you're "sitting on the patio?" Of course they don't. That line from a Verizon ad that exemplifies how useless Twitter can be, especially when used incorrectly. I would contend it's Twitter's own fault because they ask the wrong questions like: "What are you doing?" Or "What's Happening?"

If that's the wrong question, what are the right questions? While I'm not entirely sure there is one right question, I will submit that if you think about answering any of the following, you will serve yourself and your network better:

What value do you have to offer your network now?

What information can you share that your network needs?

What interesting links, quotes, or ideas would you like to share?

How can the project you are working on be a potential solution for others?

What is it that you love most about what you're doing?

What type of people may benefit from what you're doing now?

Can you make us laugh?

Can you make us think?

What exciting news happened in your day, or with your business, that you would like to share?

These are just questions that I ripped off the top of my head. You can see that they are value focused. That value should be for others and a little bit for you too.

You'll need to find the right balance between adding value for others and making sure you're getting some for you. Chris Brogan (author of Trust Agents and Social Media 101) suggests that the "golden ratio" is 10-1. For every 10 posts he makes, 9 will be to or about others and 1 will be promoting www.thirdtribemarketing.com, his books or his upcoming speaking engagements aka the stuff he gets paid for.

I have also heard from others that this "golden ratio" is 12- 1, 7-1 and 5-1. I'm not sure which one is the RIGHT answer, but you can tell it's a LOT more about others than it is about you.

Another important thing about status updates is making sure people see them. So many people have social media on a to-do list and get to it when they get to it. While it may be convenient to do your social media at 11 p.m. on a Saturday evening when everyone is asleep at your house, it's not effective. Most all sites rotate their content as new content is created. If you post on a Saturday night thinking your network will see it on Monday morning, you are mistaken. The only chance that they will see it then is if no one posts in their network. And if that's the case, you can bet they have a ᴛɪɴʏ network.

You need to post when people are going to actually see it! Facebook does a good job of showing you when people in your network are online. (The number next to the "chat" box on the lower right hand corner is the indicator).

LinkedIn is a bit more of a crapshoot, but the nice thing about that tool is that they send weekly updates to all members and your connections will be get your status updates in that message.

Twitter has hot times and less hot times. It's busy at the beginning of the work day, right after lunch and in the early evening. Since we live in a world with multiple time- zones, it appears busy all day. This is why it's important to know where your prospects are geographically so you can make sure your message hits them at the right time.

It's okay to share your message more than once. I recommend posting it at the various times because different people will be on at different times. Try re- wording it and posting it again.

One last caveat about status updates. While going negative may yield some responses, think about the types you're getting. Hopefully, before you set out on your social media campaign, you decided what you wanted to get from it. On that list should be the types of responses you want. It has been my experience that negative attracts negative. I will leave it to you to decide when you have had enough of that in your life.

I told you I would get back to this.

I Recommend Writing Recommendations

If someone does great work with or for you, do you take the time to recommend them? A well written recommendation can help the recommendee and the recommender.

Let's assume a co-worker kicks butt on a project with you. Sure you are likely to thank them, and maybe even tell their boss, but did you add it to their social networking profile? That's where it can be of most value to them. Fast forward 6 months and they are looking for a new job (through no fault of yours of course.) Prospective employers are highly likely to look at profiles of future employees.

Your recommendation may help them get the job.

Has a vendor or supplier under-promised and over- delivered? In addition to paying that invoice on time, post an endorsement for them. Your endorsement could help them land new business and new business partners.

Quick Guidelines on Recommendations:

A good recommendation should flow through you. Only write rec-

ommendations that are genuine. Try to note something specific. "He's a nice guy" Does not tell other readers very much.

Recognize that recommendations will stay online for ALL to read.

Keep 'em positive.

Spell and grammar check your recommendation. A well written recommendation says a lot about you too. Oh, and a poorly written one may say even more.

Write them without expecting anything in return.

Have you taken the time to endorse your suppliers, clients, friends, and others who have helped you along your way?

What do you do when someone asks you to write an recommendation you would prefer not to write?

Personally I let them know I am not comfortable doing it. Perhaps we don't have enough shared experience for me to write them a good one. Worse, maybe we have had a bad experience. Nobody would want that written on their profile. I am often miffed at the number of requests I get for this from people I barely know. Sure it's important to ask for what you seek, but be cognizant of whom you are asking.

The best thing about social media is how mobile it's become. Just like you, right?

I'll Like My Social Media To Go, Please aka Get A Smart Phone Dummy

Social media is so hot because it allows us to stay connected to the world around us. This world involves not only our current business network, but family and friends, as well as people we have yet to meet. From a business and job seeking perspective, these connections are priceless.

What's even cooler is how many of the sites are so compatible with mobile technology. You are 100% missing out if you don't have a smartphone. Get one. Get one now! I hear people say "I don't want to be tethered to my phone" or "no one needs to be that connected." That's old world thinking. Dinosaurs are old world and you know how well things worked out for them.

What makes social media on the go so valuable is that we have moved fully into the now generation. They called generation X "the instant gratification generation." As a senior delegate of that cohort, I can tell you things moved slow for us, relative to what happens now.

Smartphones allow you to do status updates, as you think of them. You can read and comment on others as well. Savvy users can actually check out real-time conversations that are taking place about them, their brand, their competition, or anything else that matters. This instant information, wherever you are, whenever you are there, is valuable. Couple that with the fact that you don't have to lug around your laptop to have this interaction and it becomes priceless.

You don't have to get on the smartphone train because I said so. Don't worry about the fact that in 2009 phone manufacturers produced more phones with a qwerty style keyboard than the traditional phone style.

If you want to see where business is heading, one only needs to look where the kids of today are. They are online on social media sites with their smartphones. Why, because it pays to be connected RIGHT NOW!

You're going to end up putting a lot of information on these sites, so remember

Be Careful What You Show Online

It's such a paradox to run around talking about "we are afraid of identity theft," and then have sites that have our address, photo, and phone number on them. Really? How afraid could we possibly be? Why not just post your bank account and social security # there too? Seems like that would make it easier.

While I am not particularly concerned about identity theft (you want it, you can have it) I do take some caution with what I post online. I have a handful of different passwords that I use for the sites I frequent and I am mindful that the sites, that have my address, are secure[11] and not public facing. Still, that information is a little too accessible from time to time.

You have seen Google Earth, right? People can punch in your address and then look at a satellite view of your house that updates about every 15 minutes. FREAKY!

If you buy stuff online, use a credit card that is specific for that purpose. One that if "lifted" will only cost you hundreds as opposed to thousands of dollars until you can get it straightened out. You can call, when sites ask for your social security number. The likelihood of the person on the end of the line being devious is about the same as someone hacking your internet transmission. But this option may make you feel better.

Be mindful of who is in your network. I am not saying do a full background check on everyone you allow in, but keep your eyes open. If someone sends you a note that sounds odd, believe that it may be. A friend of mine is out $400 because he tried to help another friend get back from England after having his wallet stolen. The rub was, the guy was never in England and still has the exact same wallet. If you receive messages like this, check into them before sending checks to them.

It's a really big World Wide Web. Be careful on it.

Here's a real life example of why it's important to "think before you post."

Thoughts On Webtegrity

I commented on a photo I had uploaded to Facebook, from my phone, during a training session Charlie and I led… The photo has an interesting story. When I was chatting with the audience, before we started, I noticed a guy checking some old photos out. When I asked him about them, I was surprised when he said "I just bought them." I was intrigued.

"Why" I asked.

He proceeded to tell me a story about wanting to be reminded that lots of people have suffered through hardships and made it past the difficulties. I told him that it would be fun to make up stories about the people in the photos and we proceeded to do so. The resulting misunderstandings led to some laughs during the presentation.

Fast forward 80 minutes. I am demonstrating how easy it is to take Facebook with you. I knew that I was going to use one of his photos as my example.

I picked a picture of a young couple (likely brother and sister) and uploaded it instantly to my Facebook. To keep the earlier joke alive, the only comment I made was "This is a photo of my uncle. He was hung."

I received some fast comments on it. Some asked why, some made jokes, some contemplated the meaning of the word "hung." It was fun stuff to read. I commented back that I needed to do a little more digging before I could definitively state what sort of "hung" he was.

Within 17 hours of posting I realized a few things:

1. People will believe a lot of what you post online.

2. While deception is easy, it doesn't make it right.

3. Your friends on Facebook really want to know about trivial things in your life.

4. Creating an interesting "story" on Facebook was a good way to drive eyeballs to my blog.

5. Coming clean feels better.

I wonder how long I could have let this go and how many stories could have been told.

For me, the lesson on "webtegrity" and the laughs was certainly worth the upload. I thank the people who were concerned and enjoyed those who made jokes.

I am fortunate that my little deception didn't appear to hinder any future dealings.

Sometimes these sites "jump the shark." You do remember when Fonzie jumped the shark on "Happy Days," right?[12]

When To Invest In A New Social Media Site

Right now, it's a land grab. New sites are popping up all over the web. Most of these sites promise more connections, being easier to use, and better functionality. Do they deliver on that promise? Some do, some don't.

More importantly, how do they get you to move from one to the next? Think about the amount of time you invested in creating a profile, uploading videos, blogs, photos, and other content. What about all the friends/followers or connections you added? Can you just up and leave them?

What are your criteria for joining a new social media site? Is it just one invite from the person you believe is most in the know?

Do you have to hear about it from 5 or 6 people before you check it out?

Does it have to be on the front page of the Wall Street Journal before it gets your attention?

With all of these sites out there, we need to have a plan in place for when we will check out the supposed "next best thing." If not, you could spend hours a day chasing websites. That's not a plan for success.

Like all networking, it's important to know what your goals are. It is also important to have a couple of "experts" (I use "" because there really is no such thing at this point. Social media is like the wild, wild, west and it's darn near impossible to be an expert in something that changes daily.)

One last thing to consider is the new trend in social media which are niche sites. You can find sites that are based on your geography (like *cough* motorcityconnect.com *cough cough*) or that are designed for your specialty, or favorite hobby, and the list goes on. This can be a great way to find people with whom you have common ground. And you already know how important common ground is in building relationships.

To close this section on why networking online is important I turn to the 800 pound gorilla in the Internet world.

Googling Yourself Is Far Less Dirty Than It Sounds

I am a big fan of the concept of owning "spot 1" in your networks mental rolodex. This idea spawned from the idea of owning "spot 1" on Google.

Here's the deal, most people no longer go to the yellow pages for much of anything. They Google[13] it! And with all the emphasis on "Personal branding" you need to be sure when they Google your name or your company's name, you show up. The closer you are to the top spot on page 1, the more likely those seeking you will find you.

If you were to Google Terry Bean, you would see that 4 or 5 of the front page listings on any given day are me. That's not bad considering all of the Terry Beans there are. One is a government official and gay rights activist in Portland (that's not me.) Another is a very accomplished and touring harmonica player (not me again.) Another is a pretty talented artist (not me, but I wish it were because he is the one who owns terrybean.com.)

So what happens when you Google *you*? The more common your name, the more challenging it is to own spot 1. The inverse is also true. Google Charlie Wollborg and you'll find that he not only owns spot 1, but page 1 and page 2 and page 3.

While changing your name may be a good strategy to own spot 1, you will need to create consistent and relevant content.

Another way to advance your Googleability[14] is to think about SEO. Search Engine Optimization. This is a combination of relevant content development, usage of keywords, and old school meta tags.

My LinkedIn profile shows up as the first result. Why? Because Google trusts LinkedIn. They also trust Twitter and are playing nicer with Facebook. Social media sites are full of rich, fresh content and that's what Google needs to survive. Make sure you are using some of these sites.

The last little trick I will share is that you will want to set up a profile/account on Google+. This is almost guaranteed to get you on the front page (unless someone with your name did it first.)

The 9 hard, fast rules of Social Media

These rules were conceived by Charlie Curve and I in 2008 and have delighted and educated audiences numerous times over the past four years.

1. Ready. Aim. Fire. Social networks reward early adopters. The rabbit wins. Every time.

2. Join all. Participate few. Stake your claim on new networks where your prospects play.

3. PBO is the new SEO. Ensure your Personal Brand is Optimized at every touchpoint.

4. There are several BE attitudes including: Don't be that guy. Social media is a conversation, not a sales pitch.

5. Feed your networks. Your network needs fresh content to survive, thrive and drive business.

6. It ROIs or it dies. Don't invest a ton of time, energy and effort into networks without understanding what you get from them.

7. Find your golden ratio. Share the megaphone and increase your own amplification.

8. Build your network before you need it. Plant, nurture and grow your networks before you expect to harvest.

9. Tools are not tactics. A scalpel doesn't make you a surgeon. Hire the experts.

So you now have a great understanding of networking face to face as well as online. What's left to learn? It's time to become the master. All the networking in the world doesn't amount to a hill of beans (yeah, I said it) if you don't understand this:

You After Connecting

How To Separate Yourself From Most People You Just Met

If you have been to your share of networking events, you probably already know the answer to this. FOLLOW UP! Why is it so difficult for people to do? It doesn't take that long. It makes you look professional. Heck, it may even get you MORE BUSINESS. I say avoid follow up like the plague.

Just kidding. You totally want to follow up with people that you may want a relationship with in the future. That's great news. Why? Because there are lots of people, who you will meet at an event, with whom there will be no future relationship. The key is to realize that not only is that okay, it's preferred. You really don't want to follow up with everyone. Not saying you can't, but there isn't really a need to do so. Know who you need to meet (that sounds familiar, right?), and know that it's unlikely that everyone you met can help you meet them.

When you are meeting people do your best to find out a little something personal about them. That can be their favorite fruit, coffee, candy, or fast food joint. This way, when you send them a follow up, it can be a little more custom for them. This very small act (gift card or apple or whatever you have to offer) will show them that you took the time to pay attention to them. So many people don't. How many times do you pass someone who asks "How are you doing?" and by the time you answer they're out of earshot? Don't be like that. Be engaged. Be in the moment. Listen to the answers when you ask someone a question.

Use that information and these skills to separate yourself from the others they will meet. Proper follow up procedures will be discussed later on in this section.

You already know how important it is to follow up, but do you know when to do it?

The people who really stand out are the ones who reach out on the same day to acknowledge your new relationship. Most times that happens via email. And that's just fine. I remember getting a note at about 11 pm from someone I had met 3 hours earlier at an evening mixer. I was duly impressed with the quickness and content of her note. That's a great way to demonstrate what kind of prompt person you are.

Follow up doesn't have to happen in the same day. In fact, as long as it happens within 72 hours, you are on the right track. Why 72 hours? If it gets longer than that, people may not have as fresh of a memory of you. With the barrage of email most of us get, we want to make sure we have some "name recognition" when they see our name in the "from" line.

Here's the reality, following up with someone 2 weeks after you met them, is still better than not following up with them at all.

Determining The Next Steps

Ever think about the pantheon of ways we have to interact with one another? We can talk on the phone. We can exchange messages through any number of online sites. We have email and texting. And you remember actually writing letters, right? We also have face to face meetings. Would you like to meet for coffee, cocktails, lunch, or simply at your office?

The point to all of this is, since we have all of these different ways to connect, how do we determine when to use which tool? Quick point, don't overlook the value of asking your network: "What's your favorite way to communicate?" and use that methodology for them.

It really comes down to two things:

What sort of relationship do you intend to have?

How much time do you have to invest in this type of relationship?

If you believe the individual may be a good connection for you and/or your associates in the future, a phone call or coffee may be in order. The same is true if you think you may be able to add some value for them.

If you believe the synergies are the type where you foresee you working together often, maybe a lunch is on the docket.

In either scenario, you really do need to figure out how you two can play together. A nicely crafted email, that asks them what they do and what they believe you two can create together, followed with your thoughts on the same topics, is a great place to begin.

What The Follow Up Note Should Say

Who you are

Where you met

What you talked about

Ask them for the meeting

If you and I met at a Motor City Connect meeting, and we talked about the idea of me doing some training for your company, my follow up note would look like this:

Good day Z-

It was a pleasure to meet you this past Tuesday at the Royal Oak meeting of Motor City Connect. I was the one who was talking about the ways that networking can really help you get connected to both your ideal clients and ideal business partners. We spoke briefly about the idea of me talking to your staff about some best practices effective networkers use to make the right connections. I would love to continue that conversation and confirm that this makes sense for both of us.

Would you be available for a quick conversation at 2:00 on either Thursday, February 18 or Friday the 19th? Please let me know which of these times work best for you or feel free to send me a time/date that does.

Thank you so much for your time and consideration. Be connected-

Terry Bean

PS, you can learn more about the type of training I do by clicking http://trybean.com.

See how the note is quick and to the point? It's not a ton of fluff and it gets to the heart of the matter. The reality is people are very busy. Tell them what you want them to know, ask them if they are open to having the conversation, and leave the ball in their court. You will also want to be sure to read the section on "Following up on your follow up."

The Personal Touch Always Wins

This section can be short and sweet, since the title tells you everything you need to know.

Sure you can send an email blast to all of the people you just met. Heck, maybe you will be kind enough to bcc everyone so they don't get everyone else's address (I said maybe, but please follow this best practice and BCC/blind carbon copy people if you are sending a mass mailing.) But here's the thing, that's not personal. That's not how you build relationships with *individuals*. It really doesn't even work for groups.

Take the time to write them a note. A hand written, self addressed, and regular old stamp wins. Can't do that? Have your assistant (or you) run it through the mail machine with a typed address. The company, Send Out Cards[15], offers a great way to stay connected and comes in a close third. Emailing them a link to something that may be of interest and a personal note is also high on the list. Visiting any of their numerous networking profiles, and dropping a note or asking to connect, is a decent fifth place strategy. A quick phone call that thanks them and reminds them of the discussion is also good and if you actually get to speak to them may be the best one yet. An email that does the same is next. A quick text message saying thanks is pretty low. A bland email that is nothing but prattle about your offering comes in last place, right next to spam.

The more you can make your communiqué relevant to your interaction, and potential for next steps, the better.

It's important to have an intention for your actions. When you know

131

what you want to get, it makes it easier to communicate. In the "just met you at a networking event" scenario, it's likely that you'll want to set up a follow-up meeting. That is your intention. You know that your goal is to get that meeting. As such, your message to them should include times/dates of when you can meet AND asking them if they're open to it. The example I shared in the section "**What your follow up note should say**" will help give you some ideas.

Enacting Your Foul Up System

We discussed earlier the need for a follow up system and how important it really is. Here's the truth, if you aren't going to use it, the best follow up system in the world won't make a blip of difference. So the key in follow up, like in so many other areas, is to actually ACT.

Interestingly, I just looked at the section header and I seem to have written the wrong word. Where I should have written the word "follow" I have written the word "foul." Good thing too. Otherwise this would have been the shortest section yet.

The best way to foul up your system is to not actually use it.

Following Up On Your Follow Up

You've made the call. You got their voicemail. Now what? You wait for them to call back. Or, if you're proactive, you schedule a time to make the call again. Same thing goes with e-mail, text message, twittering, Facebook, and all of the other tools.

We live in an "I'll get to it when I do" society. If we didn't, TiVO and DVR wouldn't exist. We would watch programs when they were on, as opposed to when we feel like it. Don't get me wrong, I am all for the "when we feel like it" approach. It works out well for me too. The challenge is that when we all operate on the "when we feel like it" schedule, things won't get done by others when WE feel like having them done. It makes it a little tough to get things completed.

As such, you need to know what it is you want accomplished and when the deadline is. If it's simply a matter of scheduling a first meeting to network with someone new, that's probably not as pressing as finishing a collaborative assignment on time.

When we are working together, or even just trying to work together, there ends up being a lot of communication between us. As such, we need to have a good strategy in place.

Based on the timeline, you may need to call/e-mail a couple of times a day for really pressing matters. In other situations it is okay to leave a message every 6 days. Remind them why you are trying to reach them and make sure that it is not just "urgent" for you.

I think the window that shows Important and Urgent needs to go here. Here is is:

	Urgent	Not Urgent
Important	**I** - Crisis - Pressing Issues - Deadlines - Meetings	**II** - Preparation - Planning - Prevention - Relationship building - Personal Development
Not Important	**III** - Interruptions - Some mail - Many popular activities	**IV** - Trivia - Some phone calls - Excessive TV/Games - Time wasters

Be Connected
How Do You Know If The Networking You're Doing Is Valuable?

Hopefully you have a specific purpose detailed, as well as a desired outcome, for each event you attend. You do have those, right? If so, go ahead and skip this section. I double dog dare you.

We know why we are going to events: to strengthen the relationships we have and create the new ones that we will need. That is the purpose. This is why it is important to not only RSVP, but to check the RSVP list before attending.

Outcomes are going to be a little different for everyone. I was at a meeting 2 days ago and Bjorn Olson said that as long as he meets one person with whom he wants to follow up (I love the way he words this because it is so relationship focused) he considers the event a success. Renee Howarth instantly chimed in that she agrees with him, but that her boss at the fortune 500 company didn't see it that way. They ask the same questions:

Did you sell anything?

How many appointments did you set?

Did you get any good leads?

Sure these are all important questions, but we don't go to networking events to sell, we go to network. While it is good to be able to set some follow up meetings while at an event, it is unlikely they will be sales calls on the first meeting. Networking takes time, because it's really not networking. It's not just making a connection. It's relationship building.

The caveat is you need to be clear on who you want to build those relationships with. When you know who they are, you'll have to figure out what events they attend. Networking is time consuming. When your target audience isn't at the same events you are (or at the very least accessible through the contacts you'll meet) you are wasting time. Time wasted in networking leads to disgruntled networkers…and they don't help anyone. Make sure you know who you seek and help others do the same.

You are the only one who can really determine what success will look like, for you, for an event. Know what your hourly rate is. Go to an event and try to determine if you will get 3-5X the value of your rate within six months.

Staying Visible To Your Network

It's important to recognize that everyone in your network needs to hear from you. What's dynamic about that is the frequency with which you communicate with them. Sometimes it depends on projects or workload. Other times it depends on how much you like each another.

There are people in your network that you need to communicate with almost daily. There are others that as long as you touch base with them semi-annually, you can keep the relationship strong. In either scenario, you need to have a plan on how to reach out to them.

The simplest and most effective way is to pick up the phone and make a call. Depending on how often you touch base, that may be time consuming. Certainly there are people with whom you love to speak. But you know any conversation with them is 30 minutes at least. What if you don't have that kind of time?

A sure fire way to stay on people's radar, while adding value to them, is to send them information that they will find useful. Everyone loves receiving mail that isn't a bill! Think about clipping a magazine or newspaper article, sticking it in an envelope, and actually mailing it to your colleague. Trust me when I tell you they will be blown away by the gesture.

A much faster way to achieve a similar effect is to email articles or links to people. While this lacks the mail feel, it still demonstrates caring and people will greatly appreciate your showing interest.

And of course there is no shortage of tagging folks on social media. It's amazing how much more efficient people have become with these tools since I first wrote this book. I love it.

In addition to things you have read, be sure to tell your network about events you think they will enjoy. Keeping them in the loop will benefit them, but if they attend events where you are, they may be just the person you need to introduce you to your next big opportunity.

How do you determine how often to communicate with folks and how do you reach out to them? Are you aware of their favorite ways to communicate? Just because you love to text doesn't mean they will too. Communication is much more effective when we understand how our audience prefers to receive it.

In Closing

I want to end this book in the same way it started, talking about the power of the ASK. Please, for the sake of you, your business, your network and us all get comfortable with this concept: **Giving us an opportunity to help you actually helps us too.**

Know You Have A Lot Of People You Can ASK

So far we have looked at the components of a good ask and for what to ask. If you've got those things down, it's now time to figure out who to ask. This is where it gets kind of fun. The reality is there are very few people you shouldn't be asking, or at least telling. Here's why:

It has been said that each person is the center of influence for about 250 people. While I agree that number may sound high to some of you, think about ALL of the people you know and have interacted with in your life:

Classmates

Teachers

Family

In-laws

Teammates

PTA members

Church sharers

Friends

Work colleagues

Neighbors

Club members

Bankers, store clerks, wait staff and the list goes on... and on.

Obviously you are not going to have outstanding relationships with every one of these people, but I bet you have good relationships with people in each of these groups. This is relevant because it shows you "who" out of your "network" you can ask. Hopefully you noticed that these people really aren't outside of your network at all.

What's really cool about it is, since we are all networking together, these people are now a part of all of our networks.

There are two reasons that asking multiple people is of benefit. The first one will be covered greatly in the next piece. The second one is you don't know who someone else knows. The person could be connected to exactly the person you need to meet. Asking allows you to find out whether or not the people you know can connect you to the people you want to know, through the people they know. Yeah, go ahead and read that again.

It's important to help the people whose help you are seeking. My favorite networking question of all time comes from Bob Burg. It is "How would I recognize if someone I am speaking with is a good referral for you?" Ask that. Ask that often. It's a great conversation starter. When someone is asked that, they generally want to return the favor.

The other types of folks you want to ask are those who you believe would be connected to whom you seek. If you are looking to meet a specific decision maker, find out who else sells to them. If they have an assistant, get to know them. Use tools like LinkedIn to find out about their hobbies or other things that may be of interest to them. It's funny how relationship building and stalking can be so closely related. Evidently, I need to work on my definition of funny.

We live in a world that has ***six degrees of connectedness. You should be able to contact anyone in this country within four calls. Don't get me wrong, you certainly need to make the first call count, but it can be done.

If you ever want to know who to call first, feel free to reach out to me (and we won't even count that call.)

***I have a TED talk named 6 Degrees of Connectedness that talks about the 6 areas of life you need to be connected to: Self, Others, Technology, Universe, Planet and Bliss (not in that order)

5 Tips For A Good ASK

At MCC[16], we use the term "ASK" as opposed to "30 second commercial" or "elevator pitch." Why? Those concepts are anti-quated and we have yet to hold an event with either a stopwatch or in an elevator. Besides, if the ask is done correctly, the person with whom we are speaking will know exactly what type of work we do. It's your job to BRIEFLY cover that in the ask.

By the time you read this, you should have a very good idea how to create a new and significantly improved ask for yourself.

A good ask should connect you with exactly what you seek. I am not saying it will do so every time, but your odds of making the right connection will certainly increase if you follow these guidelines.

Start with your Name, your role, and for whom you do it. It should be one quick, short sentence.

My name is Terry Bean and I am the CNO (Chief Networking Officer) of Networked Inc.

Next should be a sentence about why people do business with your company.

We are experts at infusing a networking mindset into small and medium companies so they can grow their business.

The above sentence tells you: Who, What and Why. These are certainly important elements. I have also spent about 7 seconds talking thus far. The next sentence should address how the person you are speaking with can help you. Before I get into this, I want to give you a list of things it should be:

Concise: Not that you are in a hurry, but there is no sense in giving people more information than they need. We have all been in a situation when we wished the person that was telling us every piece of minutia about their business would just go away, right? Don't be that person. Say what you have to say, but do it quickly. Our good friend, Charlie Wollborg says it this way: Titillate, don't satiate. See how brief that is?

Clear: Does it still make sense after shortening your message? If it doesn't, you may need to workshop it a little. People need to understand what it is you would like them to do for you.

Compelling: Is your request something that people think, "Hmm, that's interesting. I would like to help this person." If it's not, what are you going to do to make it so? Sure it's great that you are networking and meeting new people, but if you can't get any of them to help you, by introducing you to the people you need to meet, you would be better served spending that time cold calling. Suggestion: Relate your ask to them. That could be by offering an incentive for those who help you or by showing how what you do for your clients may benefit them.

Specific: While this seems counter-intuitive, as if it would lessen the possible number of responses you will get... know this: It will lessen the number of responses you will get. How many of us have gotten referrals that were close to what we seek? Worse yet, how many have gotten referrals that weren't even close? Sure we appreciate the effort, but who has time to track down a bunch of folks that really aren't our prospect. (If you do, call me! MCC needs some help on a handful of committees.) Make your ask as absolutely granular as you can. Don't say I am looking for someone in purchasing at GM. If you know you need to speak to Johnny Knoxville who purchases castings and works in the Warren facility. Ask for Johnny. You never know...

It's Okay to ask for help (is there an echo in here?) Tell people you are asking for their help and that you would appreciate it.

Here is an example of my ASK utilizing what we have stated here:

My name is Terry Bean and I am the CNO of Networked inc. We are experts at infusing a networking mindset into small and medium companies so they can grow their business. I would appreciate your help in connecting me with an executive at Hanson's Windows. I will help them get more business from their current base, identify future clients and strategic partner's and most importantly communicate this message throughout all of the organization.

Remember, every opportunity we have to help you, helps us. It all starts with a good ask.

I am overwhelmed with joy that you took the time to read this. I hope you found it valuable to you and I would appreciate your sharing your thoughts with me.

What did you learn?

What did you like?

Has it impacted your thinking and/or your results?

Please feel free to connect with me in any manner that is comfortable for you. You can find me on LinkedIn, Facebook, Motor City Connect, Twitter and about 17 other sites. The link underneath my name below will show you where I play online and give you my contact information.

Be connected- Terry Bean

http://yourcno.com

Acknowledgments

I would like to thank the members of Motor City Connect. The success of this group allowed me to attract many of the opportunities that I am continually grateful for today.

To my daughter Drea- You can have your daddy back. Thank you for understanding that when I say "Daddy will be with you in a second", he really means "less than three minutes". You are my inspiration and my everything.

To Stephanie, thank you for your love, support and continued belief in me. You have given me the best gift I could ever imagine in our beautiful daughter. I also appreciate you keeping me grounded and making sure my head can still fit through the door ;-)

To my mom, dad and stepmother, Karen I couldn't ask for a better set of parents. I appreciate your guidance, your parenting and your encouragement. I am who I am today because of you all.

To my good friend and partner in Motor City Connect, Charlie Wollborg, your creativity and brilliance knows no bounds. It's an honor to share the stage with you and as an added bonus, I always learn something new. A special thanks also to the wonderful team at curvedetroit.com for encouraging you to spend time with me.

I am truly honored to have Chris Brogan write the foreword for this book. I have been totally blown away with his knowledge and his dedication to sharing the majority of it so freely. He is a true master in social media and one of the finest examples of integrity I have ever seen. Thank you Chris.

Vincent Wright and the members of the group site www. bran-dergy.com. Vincent your wisdom and willingness to share it with your network every day has been my guiding light. Thank you for that.

Frank Agin and Amspirit Business Connections. Frank you gave me the blueprint on how to run a successful networking group that honors its people. You are a mentor from whom I continue to learn to this day.

Bob Burg- your books, "Endless Refferrals, "Winning Without Intimidation" and the latter ones have continued to inspire me. You have taught us all the importance of being a true "go giver". It is an honor to call you friend.

Finally, to "That Guy" at every networking meeting...thanks for being you. Without you, I wouldn't have decided there was a need for the training I built which led to the book. One request? Please be coachable.

Terry Bean

White Lake, Michigan

March 2013

About The Author

Terry's passion is helping others succeed. He is known as many things: a relationship builder, a social media expert, a connector, but most importantly he brings people together.

In 2012 Terry launched uNetworked. A disruptive marketing practice that combines his relationship marketing mastery with his partner's knowledge in digital and development.

Terry is the founder of the fastest growing networking group in Detroit, www.motorcityconnect.com. Motor City Connect began in March, 2007 and has grown to over 5500 members. The purpose of Motor City Connect is to bring Detroit area professionals together to grow themselves, their businesses and our community. Terry firmly believes all three elements are keys to business success in the now economy.

He is also the driving force behind Networked Inc., a company that provides training on the concepts and benefits of online and real world networking to numerous sales teams, groups and professionals. Terry has trained fortune 500 companies like Comcast and Gannett as well as local mom and pop shops. His trainings are inspiring, educational and very entertaining.

Terry has delivered keynote presentation at several of Metro Detroit's leading Organizations including: MI CPAs Assoc, Universities: Mich Tech U, Lawrence Tech U, Eastern Mich U, MSU, Oakland U, Walsh College, Automation Alley, Area Chambers of Commerce: Detroit Maccomb County, Troy, Birmingham, Ferndale, and Clarkston. Local organization Better Business Bureau, Automation Alley, Bizdom U. Ann Arbor Spark, Detroit Open City, Inforum, National Association of Career Women, Rotary Clubs, Optimist Clubs, Marketing groups: Adclub, 313 digital, Lunch Ann Arbor Marketing at TEDx detroit (tedxdetroit.com), National Association of Catering Executives. Interviewed by numerous people all over the country on networking and social media, trained 1000's of people individually, in groups/associations and companies ranging in size from 1 person to Fortune 500 like Comcast and Gannett and Office Depot.

Terry's early career began in technical sales in Columbus, OH selling computer networks and cabling infrastructure. This technical role led to a career as a technical recruiter with an award winning staffing firm in Columbus. Two years later, Terry set out to turn the staffing model on its ear by creating a firm that "networked" numerous staffing firms together. Terry found early success with this model and both clients and partners loved it.

Terry learned the value of networking while in Columbus. At 27 years old, Terry became the Area Director for the largest professional networking group in town.

Terry moved back to Detroit In 2000 and began working in the telecommunications field. In 2002 he helped Affinity Telecom go from $0 to sold in 2.5 years. He became the sales recruiter LDMI/Talk America where he was responsible for onboarding sales reps in 32 markets East of the Mississippi.

Terry serves on the advisory board for Operation Kid Equip, a Detroit based charity who helps school children get the school supplies they need. He also works closely with Motor City Blightbusters and the American Red Cross. It is these affiliations that led to his creating the "Blood, Sweat and Gear", #Bustup, #BrilliantDetroit and #313Dlove campaigns. Each shine the light on Detroit and encourage others to give back.

Terry has received numerous sales awards, networking awards and in 2009 he received the "Presidential Volunteer Service Award" from President Obama and the Lawrence Technical University Leaders and Innovators award in 2010. In March, 2012, Terry received the Detroit 2020 Award from WXYZ TV for his 313 D love campaign that trended worldwide.

Terry holds a B.S. in Psychology and a M.A. in Business Communications from EMU. He enjoys softball, weight training, The Simpson's and his 10 year old daughter, Drea.

Footnotes

1 Rhonda Byrne, <u>The Secret</u> (Atria Books/Beyond Words - 2006)

2 If you haven't already, sign up for Mike Dooley's daily note from the universe at www.tut.com.

3 Dr. Ivan Misner, of BNI

4 Thank you Bob Burg, for that wonderful combination of words.

5 If you don't have a LinkedIn account yet, sign up at www.linkedin.com

6 <u>Blue Ocean Strategy</u> by W. Chan Kim and Renée Mauborgne of INSEAD,

7 Shameless self promotion: Mike McClintock and I are working on a solution for this. Check out uNetworked.com.

8 Feel free to google me.

9 Okay, that's my opinion.

10 If you don't know how to quickly cut & paste text on the computer, ask the neighbor's kid.

[11] You can tell by the little padlock symbol or the s at the end of the http, in the website name.

[12] Google "jump the shark" fonzie, if you are as confused as my editor.

[13] www.google.com – just in case. Yes, the verb google is in www.Websters-Online-Dictionary.com.

[14] Not in the dictionary yet.

[15] www.sendoutcards.com

[16] Motor City Connect

Be Connected

Terry Bean

CPSIA information can be obtained at www.ICGtesting.com
Printed in the USA
BVOW070448180413

318459BV00001B/2/P